ADVANCED ENGLISH SERIES

Mechanics

For students, parents and teachers:
A straightforward way to teach and test English skills.

by C.G. Cleveland

A Breath of Fresh Air
Garlic Press

D1472310

Published by:
Garlic Press
605 Powers St.
Eugene, OR 97402

ISBN 0-931993-56-3
Order Number GP-056

www.garlicpress.com

Dear Parents, Teachers, and Students

The **Advanced Straight Forward English Series** has been designed for parents, teachers, and students. The Advanced Series is designed to measure, teach, review, and master specific English skills. The focus of this book is **mechanics**, the details of writing.

What makes this Series different?

• Various textbook series have been compared. The *Advanced Straight Forward English Series* presents the skills crucial to the mastery of mechanics as reflected in major English textbooks.

• Mechanics skills are concisely explained, practiced, and tested.

• Mastery can be measured by comparing the *Beginning Assessment Test* with the *Final Assessment Test*.

• The Advanced Series has more content and no distracting or unrelated pictures or words. The skills are straightforward.

How to use this book.

• Give the *Beginning Assessment Test* to gain a starting measure of a student's knowledge of mechanics.

• Progress through each topic. Work the exercises. Exercises can be done in the book or on a separate sheet of paper. Set a standard to move from one topic to the next. If the standard is not met, go back and refocus on that topic.

• Review practice is periodically given. Use the Review as a simple measurement of skill attainment.

• Give the *Final Assessment Test* to gain an ending measure of a student's mechanics skills. Compare the skill levels before and after the *Final Assessment Test*.

Contents

Assessment Test

A. Abbreviations. Change each of the following words into an abbreviated form. Use periods as necessary.

1.	Mistress	6.	Sunday
2.	doctor	7.	Missouri
3.	attorney	8.	anno domini
4.	voltage	9.	Eastern Standard Time
5.	avenue	10.	foot

B. Apostrophes. In the following sentences, insert apostrophes as needed.

1. Im a little teapot, short and stout.

2. How many Ts are there in this sentence?

3. This is Marys address. I dont know her sisters address.

4. The womens movement in the 60s was part of the campaign for Civil Rights.

5. The movie, *Summer of 42*, took place during the United States involvement in WWII.

C. Capitalization. In the following passages, capitalize as needed.

1. february is black history month. throughout this month, we will publish interesting moments from the history of black people in oregon. you can read about these fascinating histories every monday and wednesday on the front page of our city/region section.

2. while minnesota struggles through another losing season, doug west has emerged as one of the best young shooting guards in the nba.

3. come to taco bell for a special "cinco de mayo" treat. your hostess will be senorita donna green.

D. Identify the following symbols.

1.	:	4.	/	7.	" "
2.	( )	5.	;	8.	[ ]
3.	-- or —	6.	-		

E. Add colons, semicolons, periods, or commas as needed in the following paragraph.

Then she slowly sank down laid back her ears bared her teeth and hissed at the same time, throwing both paws out viciously. Kitty may have rested however she did not sleep. Hours after I had crawled into my sleeping bag in the silence of night I heard her working to get free. I heard the clink of her chain the crack of her teeth the scrape of her claws. How tireless she was. [Excerpt from Zane Grey's *Desert Gold*.]

F. Italics and Quotation Marks. Supply italics (underline) and quotation marks as needed.

1. She said, Be sure to dot your i's and cross your t's.
2. One of my favorite short stories is Big Two-Hearted River from the book, In Our Time.
3. Have you seen the production of Phantom of the Opera?
4. I listen each afternoon to All Things Considered on the radio.
5. Do you recall, she asked, the address?

G. Parentheses and Brackets. Supply parentheses and brackets as needed.

1. The book, printed nearly a century ago 1894, is valuable.
2. The letter was dated "April 31, 1092 sic" and signed by my father.
3. Andrew Jackson Old Hickory served as the seventh president 1829-1837.
4. "The society, Redwood Protectors RP, was established in 1922."
5. The instructions read as follows: 1 remove the top, 2 locate the bulb, and 3 replace the fuse.

H. Numbers. Which is correct?

1. one dog, one cat, three mice
   1 dog, 1 cat, 3 mice
2. 7 o'clock
   seven o'clock
3. a bargain at $4.95
   a bargain at four dollars and ninety-five cents
4. Act Three, Scene Six, line fifty-two
   Act III, Scene VI, line 52
5. Sixty two percent
   62%

I. Hyphenate where appropriate.

1. a 6 to 2 vote
2. ex mayor
3. hot dog buns
4. everyone is present
5. anti communist
6. thirty three
7. all out manhunt
8. all right
9. three quarters of an inch
10. mother in law

J. Dashes. Supply dashes as needed.

1. Lettuce, tomato, cheese everything on my hamburger, please.
2. It was obvious who would object that the award was not deserved.
3. I like this version "interpretation," if you will of the song.

Abbreviations

An **abbreviation** is a shortened form of a word or a phrase, most often followed by a period.

Titles

In formal writing, most abbreviations should be avoided. The exception is in the use of titles with names. For example:

> **Mr.** Jones, **Mrs.** Rivera, **Ms**. Kobayashi, **Dr.** Armand

or in trailing titles such as:

> Sam Eckard, **Jr.**; Donna Chou, **M.D.**; Robin McDougall, **Esq.**

Also notice that these titles are capitalized.

The following is a list of common and not-so-common abbreviations of titles which precede a name, and the titles they represent.

Mr.	mister
Messrs.	more than one mister
M.	monsieur (mister in French-speaking countries)
Mrs.	mistress or married woman
Mlle.	mademoiselle (unmarried woman in French-speaking countries)
Mme.	Madame (married woman in French-speaking countries)
Ms.	generic title for all women, married or unmarried
Sr.	Señor (mister in Spanish-speaking countries)
Sra.	Señora (married woman in Spanish-speaking countries)
Dr.	doctor
Rev.	reverend
Gen.	general
St./Ste.	saint (male/female)
Maj.	major
Sgt.	sergeant
Pvt.	private
Pres.	president
Gov.	governor
Atty. Gen.	attorney general
Hon.	honorable (used for courtroom judges)

Trailing titles that are used for scholastic or honorary degrees must not be used with beginning titles. Never use Dr. Edmund Gray, M.D., for instance. The following is a list of common and not-so-common abbreviations which follow a name, and the titles they represent.

M.D.	medical doctor
Ph.D.	doctor of philosophy
M.B.A.	master's in business administration
LL.D.	doctor of laws (lawyer)
D.D.S.	doctor of dental science (dentist)
M.L.S.	Master of Library Science (librarian)
Pharm.D.	Doctor of Pharmacy (pharmacist)
Esq.	esquire (applied to lawyers in U.S.)

Some trailing titles can be used in conjunction with titles which precede the name; e.g., **Dr.** John Anderson, **Jr.**

Ret.	retired
Jr.	junior
Sr.	senior
2nd	the second (instead of junior) or **II**
3rd	the third (after junior) or **III**

Exercise A.   Change the following names to accommodate abbreviated titles as if you were addressing a formal letter.

1.   The wife of Mr. Collins

2.   Judge Allen Baker, junior

3.   Mademoiselle Jordache and her mother

4.   Doctor of Medicine John D. Smith

5.   Mister Dobbs who is a minister

6.   Richard Browning who is a dentist

7.   Mary Louise Simpson, chief executive officer (marital status unknown)

8.   Mister Cabrillo's wife while in Spain

9.   Major General Koop who has retired

10.   Joan of Arc who is a saint

Acronyms

An abbreviation which uses the first letter of each word or a portion of each word in a name is known as an **acronym**.

An acronym is an abbreviation of an organization, a group of people, or a governmental agency. It is often formed from the first or principal letters of each complete word in the group's name, such as in **NASA** (National Aeronautics and Space Administration). In these cases, periods are not usually necessary. The following are some common organizations and their abbreviated forms.

NAACP	National Association for the Advancement of Colored People
IBM	International Business Machines
YWCA	Young Women's Christian Association
FBI	Federal Bureau of Investigation
IRS	Internal Revenue Service
MADD	Mothers Against Drunk Driving
TWA	Trans World Airlines
POW	Prisoner(s) Of War
UNESCO	United Nations Educational, Scientific, and Cultural Organization
NATO	North Atlantic Treaty Organization
GI	Literally, Galvanized Iron, this acronym has come to be associated with a U.S. military enlisted person.

An acronym can also be capitalized when first letters of prefixes are used.

ESP	Extra-Sensory Perception
CPR	Cardio-Pulmonary Resuscitation

Some acronyms and abbreviations have become words in their own right. These words do not contain periods and are not capitalized. The acronym is made from portions of several words.

sonar (**so**und **na**vigation **r**anging)

radar (**ra**dio **d**etecting **a**nd **r**anging)

radio (**radio**telephonic instrument)

awol (**a**bsent **w**ithout **l**eave)

tv (**t**ele**v**ision)

amtrac (**am**phibious **trac**tor)

rad (**rad**ical)

Exercise B.   What do the following acronyms mean? Try to guess from the clues given. You are encouraged to use the dictionary if you don't know.

1. YMCA (an organization providing shelter to men)
2. UN (a group of countries in the world)
3. USA (a group of states in North America)
4. UNICEF (an agency dedicated to worldwide health and nutrition)
5. USSR formerly unified Russia of the twentieth century)
6. DAR (a woman descendent of families living in America during the Revolutionary War)
7. RBI (a baseball term)
8. AAA (car insurance group)
9. R & R (term for vacation)
10. PLO (a Middle East extremist group)
11. HMO (health group)
12. CIA (federal espionage group)
13. RN (an occupation in the medical field)
14. IOU (a reminder of a debt)
15. NBC (a communications company)

Exercise C.   Decide which words in the following sentences can be shortened into acronyms.

1. I led the fund-raiser in our town for multiple sclerosis.
2. We danced at the Veterans of Foreign Wars hall.
3. My friend's father was a missing-in-action soldier in Vietnam.
4. Thank goodness it's Friday!
5. I read Leon Uris' book *Queen's Bench Seven* twice.
6. The European Economic Community includes France.
7. Did you know that monosodium glutamate is a preservative for foods?
8. There were many programs on television last month about unidentified flying objects.
9. My brother was never absent without leave while in the Navy.
10. Where is the center of gravity on this aircraft.
11. Lonnie's psychology term paper is about extra-sensory perception.
12. What is Babe Ruth's lifetime runs batted in.
13. I prefer news on National Public Radio to news from Columbia Broadcasting Systems.
14. All radio stations are licensed by the Federal Communications Commission.
15. What is your zone improvement plan code?

North American States and Provinces

States and provinces can be abbreviated two ways: (1) as a shortened version of the original word, and (2) without periods for the U.S. Post Office.

Alabama	Ala.	AL	Nebraska	Nebr.	NE
Alaska		AK	Nevada	Nev.	NV
Alberta	Alt.	AB	New Brunswick		NB
Arizona	Ariz.	AZ	New Hampshire	N.H.	NH
Arkansas	Ark.	AR	New Jersey	N.J.	NJ
British Columbia		BC	New Mexico	N. Nex.	NM
California	Calif.	CA	North Carolina	N.C	NC
Colorado	Colo.	CO	North Dakota	N.Dak.	ND
Connecticut	Conn.	CT	Nova Scotia		NS
Delaware	Del.	DE	Ohio		OH
District of Columbia		DC	Ontario	Ont.	ON
Florida	Fla.	FL	Oklahoma	Okla.	OK
Georgia	Ga.	GA	Oregon	Ore.	OR
Hawaii		HI	Pennsylvania	Penn.	PA
Idaho		ID	Puerto Rico		PR
Illinois	Ill.	IL	Quebec	Que.	PQ
Indiana	Ind.	IN	Rhode Island	R.I.	RI
Iowa		IA	Saskatchewan	Sask.	SK
Kansas	Kans.	KS	South Carolina	S.C.	SC
Kentucky	Ky.	KY	South Dakota	S. Dak.	SD
Louisiana	La.	LA	Tennessee	Tenn.	TN
Maine		ME	Texas	Tex.	TX
Manitoba	Man.	MB	Utah		UT
Maryland	Md.	MD	Vermont	Vt.	VT
Massachusetts	Mass.	MA	Virgin Islands		VI
Michigan	Mich.	MI	Virginia	Va.	VA
Minnesota	Minn.	MN	Washington	Wash.	WA
Mississippi	Miss.	MS	Wisconsin	Wis.	WI
Missouri	Mo.	MO	West Virginia	W. Va.	WV
Montana	Mont.	MT	Wyoming	Wyo.	WY

Names and Nicknames

Names are sometimes abbreviated or shortened. Good manners dictate that this practice be done at the discretion of the name bearer. This kind of abbreviation is also known as a nickname.

Charles	Chas.	Charlie	Chuck	
Kathleen	Kate	Kathy	Kit	Lena
Margaret	Peggy	Peg	Meg	Maggie
Alexander	Alex	Al	Lex	

Dates, Times, and Measurements

Months: Jan. Feb. Mar. Apr. May Jun. Jul. Aug. Sep. Oct. Nov. Dec.

Days: Sun. Mon. Tues. Wed. Thurs. Fri. Sat. (or Su M Tu W Th F Sa)

Time: A.M. or a.m. (*ante meridiem*), after midnight and before noon. P.M. or p.m. (*post meridiem*), after noon and before midnight.

Zones: E.S.T., eastern standard time; P.S.T ., pacific standard time; M.T., mountain time; G.M.T., Greenwich mean time

Measurements: in., inch; ft., foot/feet; yd., yard; mi., mile; lb/lbs or #, pound(s); oz., ounce; doz., dozen; gal., gallon; qt., quart; pt., pint; tsp, teaspoon; tbs/tbsp, tablespoon; l., liter; m., meter; ml, milliliter; mm, millimeter; km, kilometer; sq., square; long., longitude; lat., latitude; amt., amount

Degrees: F, Fahrenheit; C, Centigrade

Directions: S, south; N, north; E, east; W, west

Places: St., street; Av./Ave., avenue; Bl./Blvd., boulevard; Pl., place; Rd., road

Ships: SS, steamship; FS, flagship; PT boat, propeller torpedo boat

Money: $ or dol., dollar; ¢ or ct., cent

Exercise D. Use your knowledge of dates, times, and measurements to answer these questions.

1. Shorten your name in as many ways as possible. If your name is hard to abbreviate, then use the name of someone in your family or of a friend.

2. Abbreviate your birthdate along with your height and your weight.

Explanatory Notes and Note-taking

The following abbreviations are used primarily in scientific papers and explanations. Although some are used in speech (*i.e.* and *et al.*), most are used in writing. Explanatory abbreviations are often used within parentheses or brackets.

i.e.   *id est* (that is; in other words)

   Mary likes Tommy and Eddie and Charles (**i.e.**, Mary likes boys).

e.g.   *exempli gratia* (for example)

   Most fruit (**e.g.**, cherries and peaches) are grown on trees while many vegetables (**e.g.**, potatoes and turnips) are grown under ground.

in re   in the matter of; regarding

   I am answering your letter of 2/12/93 **in re** your request for more books.

op cit.   *opere citato* (in the work cited)

ibid.   *ibidem* (in the same work—used to indicate that a particular citation is from the same work as the one cited directly before)

et al.   *et alibi* (and other people not named)

   Attendees from surgery were John Smith, M.D., Sara Ferguson, M.D., Ph.D., D.H. Eddleman, R.N., **et al.**

etc.   *et cetera* (and other related things)

   Discussions at the national defense conference centered on cutbacks, layoffs, restructuring, **etc.**

Shorthand can be useful in taking quick notes over the phone or while listening to a lecture. Most note-taking abbreviations are followed by a period. Here are some standard abbreviations which are easy to decipher.

@	at	**F.Y.I.**	for your information
&	and	**inc.**	incorporated
&c.	et cetera	**incl.**	including
abbrev.	abbreviation	**info.**	information
appt.	appointment	**lft**	left/lift
apt.	apartment	**lt.**	light
assn.	association	**ltd.**	limited
assoc.	associate(s)	**ltr**	letter
attn.	attention	**mfr.**	manufacturer
C.O.D.	cash on delivery	**msg.**	message
corp.	corporation	**P.O.**	post office
corresp.	correspondence	**P.S.**	post script
ex.	example	**rt**	right
fridge	refrigerator	**std.**	standard

Exercise E. Rewrite the following passages. Change all abbreviations to their formal length.

1. Dear Monica, Wait for me @ sch. in the hallway next to Mr. Frasier's rm. I need to go over the assnmt for quest. on the exam to be held on Tues. Also, re Sat. night: I've incl. Betty and Joan in the plans. Will you be wearing your blue dress, blue heels, blue earrings, etc.? Well, gotta run. I have an appt @ the dentist in twenty min. Yrs truly, Becky.

2. Col. John Jones, ret., visited his home state of Ala. last mo. to meet his bro. for the 1st time in 17 yrs.

3. Barb. Adams, Atty at Law, sent msgs to the attn of all C.E.O.'s in chg of telecommunications.

4. What is the lat. of No. Calif.?

5. That co. packs tomatoes.

6. Eugene, OR, U.S.A., is in Lane Co.

7. I work on the 9th Fl. of the fed. bldg. on State St.

8. The YWCA is located next to Beans & Franks Deli.

9. On Sat. morn., a storm swept across towns from N.Y. City to Atlanta, GA.

10. The storm moved east at 50 mph and dumped 5 ft. of snow in the mtns.

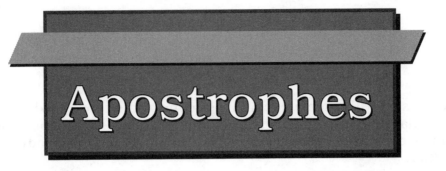
Apostrophes

*The **apostrophe** (') is used to indicate the omission of one or more letters in a word, to show possession, or to indicate plurals of abbreviations and symbols.*

Contractions

An apostrophe is used when two words are combined into one word; thereby, eliminating a letter. The apostrophe is a substitute or stand-in for the omitted letter. These contractions are best used in informal writing.

Use an apostrophe when combining a pronoun with a verb.

    I am becomes **I'm**   **You are** becomes **You' re**

Use an apostrophe when combining a verb with the negative "not."

    are not becomes **aren' t**   **do not** becomes **don' t**

Use an apostrophe to contract a proper noun with a verb in informal English.

    John is going becomes **John's going**

Omission of Letters

An apostrophe is used to indicate regional or colloquial speech styles where certain sounds are dropped. Sometimes the g from words ending in **ing** is dropped; sometimes the **a** which begins certain words is dropped.

    coming becomes **comin'**   **around** becomes **'round**

Exercise A. In the following passages from Zane Grey's *Desert Gold*, place apostrophes where appropriate.

1. "Shore, lady, Yaquis goin home," replied Ladd gently. "An considerin our troubles, I reckon we ought to thank God he knows the way."

2. My names Belding. Im the inspector and Id like to know what you mean by taking up [all] my rangers land claims.

Possessive Pronouns

To show possession with pronouns, an apostrophe and **s** are added to the end of an indefinite singular pronoun. Indefinite pronouns include such pronouns as **everybody, everyone, anybody, anyone, somebody, someone, one, other, somebody else, someone else,** or **another.**

An apostrophe and **s** are never used with personal pronouns such as **ours, mine,** or **yours.**

Is this anybody**'s** seat? Yes, this seat is someone else**'s.**

Possessive Nouns

To show possession or ownership with nouns not ending in **s,** an apostrophe and **s** are added to the end of proper nouns.

Mary's lamb or **Chevrolet's** Nova or **Halley's** Comet

The **'s** is also added to common nouns whether singular or plural.

My **dog's** bone (singular noun)
The **children's** hour (plural noun)

To show possession or ownership with singular nouns ending in **s**, there are two rules to follow:

If the noun has only one syllable, use **'s**; i.e., boss's, glass's, Jess's.

If the noun has more than one syllable and ends in **s**, you can usually use an apostrophe alone at the end of the word; i.e., Thomas', seamstress'.

To form the possessive of a plural noun which already ends in **s**, whether common or proper, use the apostrophe alone.

The two ribbons' colors were exact. (The colors of both ribbons)
This is a bosses' meeting only.   (The meeting of all bosses.)
But, My boss's meeting was today. (The meeting of one boss.)

12

To show joint ownership of both parties of a compound noun, add **'s** to the last word only. This indicates that the *thing* being modified belongs to both or all parties stated.

Bill & Kristen**'s** home   The home of Bill and Kristen [together]

Amos & Andy**'s** television show   The show of [both] Amos and Andy

To show separate ownership of both or all parties of a compound noun, add **'s** to each word. This indicates that the *thing* being modified belongs to each party individually.

Ford's and Chevrolet's **V-8 engines** were popular in the 1950s. (Ford's engine and Chevrolet's engine)

Nancy's, Ellen's, and Joan's **dresses** were exactly alike. (Nancy's dress and Ellen's dress and Joan's dress)

To indicate the possessive of a compound noun used as an adjective, add **'s** to the last part.

sister-in-law**'s** house

attorney general**'s** speech

teaspoon**'s** measurement

Note: Do not confuse this rule with plural compounds which are actually used as nouns. In these instances, the first part of the compound is plural, and no apostrophe is used.

I have three sister**s**-in-law.

The last three attorney**s** general were Republican appointees.

Exercise B. Place apostrophes correctly in the following sentences. Indicate in the space provided if the 's is omitting a letter (O), or if it shows possession (P).

1. Ive learned to like goats milk. _____ _____

2. Martinas going to the Teddy Bears picnic. _____ _____

3. Youre going where? _____

4. Those little puppies tails are waggin to beat the band. _____ _____

5. Somebodys calling my name. _____

Exercise C.   Complete the following table by changing the singular word to plural, then to singular possessive, and then to plural possessive.

Singular	Plural	Singular Possessive	Plural Possessive
child	children	child's	children's
dog	dogs	dog's	dogs'
vest			
mother			
sheep			
campus			
folly			
island			
woman			
caress			
justice			
fox			
bush			
father-in-law			
person			

Plurals of Letters, Figures, and Symbols

Add 's when numerals, symbols, letters, or words are used to represent themselves as a plural noun,

> Mind your *p* 's and *q* 's.
> This card game is called Crazy *8* 's.
> Change all the *him* 's to *her* 's in the following paragraph.

It is acceptable to use   without an apostrophe to indicate the plural of a particular block of years when numerals are used.

> The 1960s were turbulent years.
> The 1980's were affluent years.

However, when used to show possession, always use 's.

> That dress reflects the 1930's style.
> This antique is representative of 1850's kitchenware.

Exercise D.   Add apostrophes to the following passages where necessary.

1. The Mexicans were hastily erecting adobe houses upon Ladds 160 acres, upon Dick Gales, upon Jim Lashs and Thornes.

2. The mid-Atlantic and Northeast coastlines were especially susceptible to the powerful Noreaster which blew in last December.

3. Itll be an easy climb to the mountains crest, but it will become difficult as you near the eagles nest.

4. Sunday is reserved for a trip to Grandmas house.

5. The only cars at the beginning of the century were Model As and Model Ts.

Exercise E.   In the following sentences, find misplaced apostrophes or words which need apostrophes, and correct them.

1. "Its a fine day today," said Betty.

2. Thats a mighty fine horse youve purchased.

3. I'd bring my blue purse, but it's clasp is broken.

4. Apples's and orange's: they're all the same.

5. "Somethin is wrong at the Applegate Farm," croaked Zeke.

6. Susans attending her brothers farewell party.

7. Grandma always says, "Mind your *P*s and *Q*s!"

8. I said that nobodys going to find you're mistake.

9. The puppies and kittens toys were lost in the fire.

10. Im an ol cowhand from the Rio Grande.

Capitalization

Capitalization of words and letters indicates the importance of specific words or letters in a particular setting.

First Words

Capitalize the first word of every sentence.

> **I** like ice cream.
>
> **Mother** told me so.
>
> **The** corn grows tall in that field.

Capitalize the first word of complete sentences after a colon.

> This is the essence of the message: **Go** to your grandmother's house after school.

Capitalize the first word in a direct quotation.

> **"Father,"** she said, "please be careful."
>
> **"Come** to my parlor," said the spider to the fly.
>
> Tony pleaded with Dad, **"Please** let me come, too."

Capitalize the first word of each line of poetry.

> I met an old man from Kent
>
> Who didn't know which way John went.
>
> So he stopped at the store
>
> Seeking directions and more
>
> Then went away quite content.

Capitalize the first word of each line in an outline.

> I. Trip to Greece
>   A. Necessities
>   1. Extra set of swim wear
>   2. Toiletries
>   3. Gifts for my sponsors
>   B. List of places to visit
>   1. Grandmother's birthplace
>   2. My music teacher's parents' home

Capitalize the first words of greetings and closings in letters.

> Dear Mom,
>
> Love, John
>
> Yours truly, Jane Kitterman

Exercise A. Complete the following.

1. Write a short poem.
2. Make a list in outline form of things to do before going camping.
3. Write a short note to your best friend.

Proper Nouns and Pronouns

Capitalize the first letter of ships, planes, spacecraft, buildings, organizations, institutions, and brand names. Capitalize adjectives only if the word is specific to the proper noun.

> **The** Garlic Press (company), *but not* a garlic press (equipment)

Specific	General
The Enterprise (spacecraft)	Del Monte peaches
Mercy Hospital	a Macy's department store
the Sears Building	Nike sneakers
the Black Panthers (organization)	black panthers (wild animals)
New York City	the city in New York

Capitalize personal names, places, and oceans.

Fido	Admiral Koop	Uncle Grant
President Clinton	Mom *but not* my mom	ex-President Bush
North Pole	Atlantic Ocean	Mr. Jones
Eiffel Tower		

Capitalize religious names, religious pronouns, and mythical deities or symbols.

Mormons	God, *but* god (secular)
Thor (the Scandinavian god of thunder)	Earth or Mother Earth
Him or Herself in reference to religious gods	the Deity, *but* a deity
Father Time	the Grim Reaper
Buddha	Christ
Mohammed	Allah
Thy, Thee, Thou	

Time Periods or Events

Capitalize the first letter of each word indicating time periods, eras, ages, epochs.

> the Dust Bowl Era, *but* an era
> the Civil War Period, *but* a period in history
> our Twentieth Anniversary, *but* an anniversary party
> the Ming Dynasty, *but* a dynasty in China

Capitalize the first letter of each word of a special event.

> Bay to Breakers Marathon
> the Super Bowl
> the Junior Prom

Proper Names: Brand, Geographical, Titles

Capitalize brand or corporate names.

> Del Monte, Snickers, General Motors, Texaco, Macintosh

Capitalize geographical and directional words when they are part of a region or place. Distinguish between directions (traveling southwest on I-5) and part of a region (Mt. Vernon National Park is in Southwest Indiana).

> Western Hemisphere, the Middle East, South Pole, The Gold Coast in Africa, the Upper Peninsula (Northern Michigan), Down East (Maine), Upstate New York

Don't capitalize geographical directions such as: the southwestern part of Arizona, the northern lights (Aurora Borealis), in western Alberta, east coast, west coast.

Capitalize the titles of books, songs, poems, articles, etc.

> *Little House on the Prairie* (book)
> *Gunga Din* (poem)
> *Mother Goose's Nursery Rhymes* (fairy tale)
> *A Midsummer's Night Dream* (play)

Exercise B. Capitalize each word which needs capitalization.

1. a tiny fuzzy bird peeked out of the nest.

2. the door opened slowly and Bob shouted, "boo!"

3. let's put this problem in perspective: one apple and one apple equal how many apples?

4. flooding was severe along the atlantic coast.

5. traffic was snarled in the eastern and western parts of the state, and in the south.

Exercise C.   Correctly capitalize the following paragraph.

In an extraordinary collaboration by detroit's automakers, general motors, ford and chrysler are discussing building jointly an electric car to meet the requirements of the clean-air law first enacted in california, and recently adopted by several northeastern states.

Italics

Italics *(or <u>underlining</u>) distinguishes words and symbols for emphasis and importance.*

Italic type is a slanted type used in printing. Desktop computers can also vary type to produce italics. For typing or handwriting, underlining serves the same purpose as italics.

Titles

Italicize (or underline) titles of: books, newspapers, periodicals, lengthy poems, plays, and musical compositions; radio programs, films, and television programs; paintings, sculptures, and works of art; ships, trains, aircraft, and spacecraft.

A Farewell to Arms (book)	the *Nautilus* (ship)
Paradise Lost (poem)	*The Thinker* (sculpture)
Citizen Kane (film)	*Applachian Spring* (musical composition)
Othello (play)	*Mona Lisa* (painting)
Apollo II (spacecraft)	*Hiawatha* (poem)
Time (magazine)	the *Starlight Express* (train)
The Barber of Seville (opera)	the *Wall Street Journal* (newspaper)

Italicize (or underline) and capitalize articles (e.g., a, an, the) at the beginning of a title only when they are part of the title itself.

Foreign Words and Phrases Not Used Frequently

Do not italicize foreign words which have become common to the English language. While spaghetti (Italian), cliché (French), zombi (African), powwow (Algonquian), and rodeo (Spanish) did not originate in the English language, they have been incorporated and are frequently used.

Reserve italics for foreign words and phrases that are not used everyday.

caveat emptor (Latin: buyer beware)	*bête noire* (French: dreaded object)
ex post facto (Latin: retroactive)	*homo sapien* (Latin: humankind)
zeitgeist (German: spirit of the times)	*magnum opus* (Latin: masterpiece)

déjá vu (French: already seen)
corpus delicti (Latin: evidence)
vis-á-vis (French: face-to-face)
raison d' étre (French: reason for being)
carte blanche (French: blanket permission)
a capella (Italian: unaccompanied music)
non compos mentis (Latin: not competent)
quid pro quo (Latin: equivalent exchange)

coup de grâce (French: final blow)
esprit de corps (French: spirit, pride)
in toto (Latin: entirely)
junta (Spanish: secret council)
sotto voce (Italian: privately)
jihad (Arabic: holy war)
shalom (Hebrew: peace)
faux pas (French: mistake)

Words, Letters, or Figures Used to Represent Themselves

The best way to illustrate this usage is through examples in context.

You cannot tell an *i* from an *e* or a *u* from a *v*.
Many people incorrectly use *there* for *their* in writing.
The *10* was crossed out and replaced with a *20*.
I cannot distinguish your *7*'s from your *1*'s.

Legal Cases and Scientific Names

Whitney vs California
Brown vs The Board of Education
Sibaldus musculus (Blue Whale)
Vulpes fulva (North American Red Fox)
Loxodonta africana (African Elephant)

Caution: Italics should be reserved for emphasis. Uncontrolled use deflates the attention that their placement tries to achieve.

Exercise A. Supply italics (underlining) as appropriate.

1. Native New Englanders add an r to words ending in a and omit the r in words ending in r. For example, sofa sounds like sofer and roller sounds like rolla.

2. Would you rather listen to Mozart's Eine Kleine Nachtmusik or Magic Flute?

3. I recently read Shakespeare's comedy All's Well That Ends Well and his tragedy Troilus and Cressida.

4. Justice Goldberg delivered the opinion of the court in Cox v. Louisiana.

5. How many s's are there in the word Mississippi?

6. The American Firefly (Photinus pyralis) is largely found east of the Mississippi River.

7. The words bourgeois and milieu have French origins.

8. National Geographic, Smithsonian, Newsweek, Science, New Yorker, and Reader's Digest arrive in the mail each month, and I read them all.

9. They worked as if they had been given carte blanche to change the world.

10. How many times have you seen Star Wars or ET?

11. Underline every 7 on the page.

12. The opposition successfully staged a coup d' état only to be overthrown six months later.

13. Voyager sent back exceptional photographs as it passed the planet Neptune.

14. Lindbergh's flight across the Atlantic in the Spirit of St. Louis took over thirty-three hours.

15. His words are a non sequitur to his actions.

16. Facetious contains the vowels a, e, i, o, and u.

17. The recent production of The Marriage of Figaro received a glorious review in the magazine Opera Monthly.

18. Many novels of intrigue are set on the Orient Express.

19. Have you read Cooper's The Deerslayer or The Last of the Mochicans?

20. Monday through Friday, we listen to Morning Edition. Saturday and Sunday, we listen to Weekend Edition.

Quotation Marks

Quotation marks *enclose all direct quotations, words used in a special sense, and some titles.*

Direct Quotations

Quotation marks enclose passages borrowed from written works and direct speech. Use double quotation marks (" ") to enclose such direct quotations.

From written work:

> In *Pudd'nhead Wilson*, Mark Twain wrote: "Training is everything. The peach was once a bitter almond; cauliflower is nothing but cabbage with a college education."

From direct speech:

> "All right," he conceded, "you win."

> She smiled and reminded him, "The next time be more prudent about your statements."

> "The next time I'll think twice before I speak so hastily about a subject that is so volatile," Henry chuckled.

As the speaker changes in a dialogue, use a new set of quotation marks. Notice also that each time the speaker changes, a new paragraph begins.

For long quotations which have more than one paragraph, use quotation marks at the beginning of each paragraph and at the end of the last paragraph.

Long quotations can also be indented on both sides or set entirely in smaller type.

Use single quotation marks (' ') for quotations within quotations.

> Elena remarked, "I don't know who said, 'Five is the winning number,' but they were right."

Titles of Chapters, Short Stories, Essays, Short Poems, Songs, Articles from Periodicals, Single Episodes of Television Shows

"Big Two-Hearted River" (short story)

"The Road Not Taken" (poem)

"White Christmas" (song)

The last chapter is entitled "Last But Not Least."

Albert Einstein published his paper "General Theory of Relativity" in 1915.

Merle Orp's "The Train Stopped with a Jerk and You Got Off" appeared in the April 1982, issue of *Humor and Such*.

Did you see the segment of *60 Minutes* entitled "Uncommon Sense"?

Definitions

The Latin abbreviation *et al.* means "and others."

The French phrase *bête noire* means "something or someone to be avoided."

Special Emphasis

Words which are technical, slang, colloquial, used in a humorous or an ironical sense, or are trade or shop jargon warrant quotation marks. The quotation marks are often equivalent to affixing the phrase "so called" to the expression.

This was purely a "wildcat" action.

I "love" your mother's cream of primrose soup.

Such a fee is really an "invisible" tax.

He wanted me to "hang-out" with the gang.

We affectionately called him "motor mouth."

With Other Punctuation

Place a comma or period inside closing quotation marks.

Our representative Marcel Smersh says, "It is easier to get forgiveness than permission."

Place a semicolon or colon outside closing quotation marks.

He spoke of "anti-heroes"; yet I remember only one in the novel: the mad and crazed professor.

Place question marks, exclamation marks, and dashes inside quotation marks when they are part of the quotation.

"Joan! Stop! Wait!"

My cousin asked, "How long have you been here?"

Place question marks, exclamation marks, and dashes outside quotation marks when they are not part of the quotation.

What pessimist said, "If at first you don't succeed, give up"?

Exercise A. Appropriately italicize (underline) or place quotation marks in the following phrases.

1. The Complete Short Stories of Mark Twain (a book)
2. Jabberwocky (poem)
3. The Saturday Evening Post (magazine)
4. A Prairie Home Companion (radio program)
5. H.M.S. Bounty (ship)
6. Lose Weight and Grow Young (tabloid article)
7. The News from Lake Woebegon (segment of a radio program)
8. The Economy and Employment Today (an address)
9. Oklahoma, Carousel, South Pacific (musical productions)
10. An Essay on Thrift (essay)
11. Raiders of the Lost Ark (movie)
12. Cleveland Plain Dealer (newspaper)
13. Modern Life (magazine section)
14. Das Rheingold (musical work)
15. Three Musicians (painting)
16. The Lottery (short story)
17. Singing in the Rain (song)
18. China Clipper (aircraft)
19. Saving: The Road to Prosperity (journal article)
20. The Last Decision (book chapter)

Exercise B. Provide appropriate italics and quotation marks.

1. Passage to India is a Walt Whitman poem from Leaves of Grass, while A Passage to India is a novel by E.M. Forster.

2. Charles Dickens' A Christmas Carol is a classic short story revisited every Christmas.

3. In Our Time, published in 1925, contains the venerable short stories: A Very Short Story, Cat in the Rain, My Old Man, Indian Camp, and Out of Season.

4. Albert Busby's article The Bees that Swarmed Los Angeles is a simple article on Apis mellifera, the common honeybee.

5. An editorial in the Register-Guard entitled Will Our Public Fund Education challenged taxpayers to invest in the future.

Exercise C. Supply necessary quotation marks.

1. Completion is impossible, said the supervisor, before the first of next week.

2. Is completion possible before next month? asked the supervisor.

3. The so-called valuable gift was nothing short of worthless.

4. Don't confuse allusion with illusion in your speech or writing.

5. Look out–look out for–, he stammered.

6. Telling a performer to break a leg is supposed to bring them good luck.

7. Your friend gives new meaning to the term space cookie.

8. Stop humming Three Blind Mice!

9. Go! shouted the official.

10. My dictionary defines ennui as boredom.

11. My brother faltered, Why–why did you say that?

12. Follow me, she whispered, and do as I do.

13. A large crowd is expected, said the conductor.

14. The conductor said, A large crowd is expected.

15. A large crowd, said the conductor, is expected.

Exercise D.

1. Write a sentence placing a question mark outside closing quotation marks.

2. Write a sentence placing a semicolon outside closing quotation marks.

3. Write a sentence placing a comma inside closing quotation marks.

4. Write a sentence placing an exclamation outside closing quotation marks.

5. Write a sentence placing a comma outside closing quotation marks.

Numbers

*Spell out **numbers** that can be written in one or two words. Use numerals (figures) to express numbers that can be written in more than two words.*

Follow these two guidelines:

after thirty-two years	after 132 years
exactly fifty dollars	exactly $49.95
one-half	24-1/2 or 2
ten thousand people	10,226 people
2 million gallons	2,194,345 gallons

The use of numbers, whether spelled out or written as numerals, varies within different disciplines. Scientific writers, technical writers, and journalists tend to have certain conventions unique to their worlds. Our intent, here, is to acknowledge those worlds, but to strike a convention for standard written English.

Remembering our beginning statements (when to spell out numbers and when to use numerals), consider:

Conventional Uses

Addresses

8 Hillview Lane #2, Eugene, OR, 97401

PO Box 27	Route 6	Apartment 24
116 First Street	12 - 142nd St.	1521 Elm Crt.

Dates

January 11, 1946	May 6th	1922-1934
1962-76	May 6 (May sixth is acceptable, too)	
4 A.D.	the 1960s	the sixties

Time

7:00 a.m.	5:23 p.m.	1600 hours
one o'clock (not 1 o'clock)		twelve midnight
three in the morning		

Pages and Divisions of Books and Plays

pages 127-132   chapter 8   exercise 2-B
Act IV, scene III, line 24 (IV, III, 24)
Matthew 13:10   volume 4

Scores and Statistics

Toronto 6, New York 4   an SAT score of 620
average age of 27   a 3-to-4 ratio

Mathematical and Technical Numbers

58 percent, or 58%   .02   longitude 23°14' E

8-1/2 or 8   2400 lbs.   32°C

Beginning of a Sentence

Twenty-seven states ratified the amendment on time.

Large Round Numbers Followed by a Word such as Million or Billion

The population of Canada is roughly 25 million.

Comparing Numbers in a Series

The report concluded that out of 226 people, only 6 were from Oregon, only 24 were from Texas, and only 103 were from Vermont.

Clarity

When two numbers are side-by-side, write out the shortest number to avoid confusion.

Please buy 97 six-cent stamps.
We need twelve 36-ounce cups.

But, punctuation can play a balancing act:

> ...of the six, five were faulty...
> ...of the original 100, 6 were red...

Ordinal Numbers

Ordinal numbers indicate order: first, second, third, twenty-seventh, etc. Ordinal numbers should be spelled out, except for dates (May 6th) or possibly addresses (110-42nd Street).

Exercise A. Correct inappropriate use of written or ordinal numbers.

1. The 2 letters were mailed June 23.
2. The IRS will receive well over 2,000,000 tax returns per day during April.
3. The buffet can serve 50 people an hour.
4. The 10th annual meeting falls on Saturday.
5. 127 people walked, 114 drove, and 40 rode their bicycles.
6. A 2/3-majority is required.
7. She has a two point five grade point average.
8. Chapter six, exercise two is difficult.
9. We have two pigs, three cows, and forty-two chickens.
10. The purchase order required 32-twelve inch rulers.
11. Make the check for two thousand six hundred and forty-eight dollars.
12. The sales tax is one dollar and 49 cents.
13. Do you watch channel twelve news at six o'clock?
14. The loan was for six and one-half percent.
15. The temperature dropped to thirty-two degrees Fahrenheit.
16. They sell packets of 12 3 1/8 inch gaskets.
17. We arrived June fourth, 1992.
18. Put it in the two and three-fourth by 6 1/2 inch book.
19. We were paid three dollars and seventy-five cents an hour.
20. The national debt is a mere four hundred billion dollars.
21. Is your birthday on the 21st or 22nd of November?
22. The game ended in a 6 to three Blue Jay victory.
23. Our appointment was for two-thirty p.m.
24. The supply made twenty-five quarter pound patties.
25. Elena has 7 siblings ranging in age from 16 to 30.

Mid-Review Test

Exercise A. What do the following abbreviations stand for?

1. e.g.
2. NBC
3. Atty.
4. DMV
5. ESP

Exercise B.   In the following exercises, abbreviate where it is appropriate.

1. Mister Jones will speak at the assembly tomorrow.
2. Janet Byers, doctor of medicine at Saint Agnes Hospital, will take doctor Monroe's calls today.
3. General John Thomas Masters, the third, retired
4. It is my pleasure to accept the invitation to senora del Mundo's party.
5. The sign on my father's door says Bradford L. Boynton, senior, esquire, attorney at law.

Exercise C. Capitalize and insert apostrophes.

1. Thomas jefferson wrote the declaration of independence in 1776. he later was elected governor of virginia and the third president of the united states. he designed monticello, his unique home pictured on the nickel.
2. Scientists won't know how much information was collected until discovery returns spartan to earth. the eight-day atmospheric research mission is scheduled to end friday with a landing at kennedy space center. Early tuesday evening, astronauts videotaped the russian space station mir as the two spacecraft passed within 350 miles of one another.

Exercise D. Insert apostrophes, italicize (underline), and use quotation marks where necessary.

1. My Fair Lady is the musical version rendition, if you will of George Bernard Shaws Pygmalion.
2. The word holocaust comes from the Greek word meaning whole-burnt.
3. Ex-President Jimmy Carters full name is James Earl Carter.

Commas

*A **comma** separates words, phrases, and clauses.*

The comma is the most frequently used punctuation within a sentence. It is also the most frequently misused punctuation.

Approximately two-thirds of all punctuation involves the comma. In principle, the comma is a simple punctuation. It is meant to separate one word, phrase, or clause from another.

The comma is not the only punctuation that separates words, phrases, or clauses. Semicolons, colons, parentheses, and dashes also serve this function and will be discussed in the following chapters.

Introductory Elements and Transitional Expressions

Use commas to set apart terms of address.

> Please, **Dick,** don't go.
> Dear John, (in an informal letter)
> **Dana,** what do you think about this dress?

Use commas to separate introductory dependent clauses.

> **When I first get to work,** I adjust the thermostat.
> I adjust the thermostat <u>when I first get to work</u>. (no comma)

Use commas to set off transitional expressions.

> I'll have some cake. **No, on second thought,** I'll have the pie.
> Something's not right. **In other words,** let's get out of here!

Items in a Series

Commas are used to separate three or more similar items in a series, the exception being the adjective which only needs two or more words. The comma takes the place of a conjunction. The series can be composed of single words, phrases, or clauses.

Nouns:	<u>Apples, peaches, and oranges</u> are all fruit.
Verbs:	My dog <u>fetches, rolls over, and lifts his paw</u> for you to shake.
Adverbs:	The children were <u>tired, dirty, and happy</u> after their camping trip.

Adjectives in a series are followed by commas wherever they modify the same noun. These adjectives are also known as coordinate adjectives.

Adjectives:	It was a <u>close, exciting</u> game.
	It was <u>long, hard, boring</u> work.

Note: Not all adjectives in a series need a comma to separate them.

A tiny fuzzy yellow chick followed its mother across the road.

The big bad wolf blew the house down.

Phrases:	Contact the voters <u>by calling on the phone</u>, <u>by writing letters to their homes</u>, or <u>by going door to door</u>.
Clauses:	I can't determine <u>which side is up</u>, <u>which side is down</u>, or <u>which side is in the middle</u>.

Exercise A. Underline words separated by commas to form a series. Indicate whether the series represents a string of (a) nouns, (b) verbs, (c) adverbs, (d) adjectives, (e) phrases, (f) clauses, or (g) no commas necessary.

1. (   ) Thank you for your kind thoughts, your gifts, and your prayers.

2. (   ) It was a dark, stormy, and windy night.

3. (   ) Your doll is either on the stereo, in your tool box, or under the bed.

4. (   ) Candy ran, jumped, and dived into the pool.

5. (   ) I saw Jeff, Amy, Dee, Jean, and Cam at the conference.

6. (   ) The kitten was a little fluffy ball of fur.

7. (   ) I want to know what I did, what I said, or what I forgot that made her so mad at me.

8. (   ) The child's forehead felt hot, sticky, and feverish.

9. (   ) Let me know which direction to take, how many miles I'll be traveling, and how long it should take me to get there.

10. (   ) Doug read the newspaper, drank a cup of decaf, and drove to work.

Nonrestrictive Appositives

An appositive renames the noun which it modifies. A nonrestrictive appositive does not change the basic meaning of the sentence, it just gives you some additional information.

> This road, **a narrow and winding trail,** takes you to the castle.
> Surrounding the castle is a moat, **a murky and polluted swamp.**

Nonrestrictive Clauses and Phrases, or Parenthetical Remarks

When phrases or clauses are not essential to the meaning of the sentence, then we use commas to separate them from the main clause.

> **Clause:**   I spent the day studying physics, **which is my poorest subject.**
> **The main clause:** *I spent the day studying physics* stands on its own.

> **Phrase:**   Physics, **challenging my intellect,** will not defeat me.
> **The main clause:** *Physics will not defeat me* stands on its own.

Compare the restrictive (or essential) clause and phrase below which do not require commas.

> **Phrase:**   I studied Physics **on the bus home.**
> **Clause:**   Physics is a subject **that is challenging to my intellect.**

Commas are frequently used to set off extra information that is closely related to the full sentence. This information is called parenthetical because it is inserted as extra comment or explanation. The main thrust of the sentence is understandable and complete without it. But to signal its parenthetical nature, commas are used.

> This trail, **narrow and winding,** takes you to the castle.
> Surrounding the castle is a moat, **murky and polluted.**
> **Frankly speaking,** the stench was horrible.
> Locals, **some people say,** are ashamed of the eyesore.

Contrasting Elements

A contrasting element is a parenthetical remark used to counterbalance the main flow of the sentence, to provide contrast. Contrasting elements are usually short and use words like *not, but, unlike,* or *never.*

> The people, **not Congress,** voted for change.
> Martha, **not her sister,** attended Harvard.
> The vote would have been unanimous, **but for one dissenter.**
> The son, **unlike his father,** is willing to compromise.

Exercise B. Place commas wherever needed in the following passages.

1. Notwithstanding Thomas's belief which Doris shared Andrea did not appear at all during the appointed hour.

2. When Sam and his friends went outside Fido his dog was eating under the porch where he always stayed.

3. The storm was gathering on the anniversary of one of the worst storms on record the Blizzard of 1888.

4. Jane could you hand me the wrench—the one closest to the rear tire?

5. On August 6 1945 the U.S. dropped the A-bomb on Hiroshima Japan.

6. Doug prefers to go rafting not to go hiking.

7. On the other hand I think I'll go rafting too.

8. Commas used correctly avoid confusion.

9. FEMA and the American Red Cross activated emergency plans including the Emergency Broadcast System.

10. In southern Louisiana where it rarely snows two inches of snow fell last night.

Exercise C. In the following sentences, explain why the comma is placed where it is. Do the commas separate (a) series, (b) terms of address, (c) parenthetical expressions, (d) nonrestrictive clauses and phrases, (e) dependent clauses, or (f) names, dates or addresses?

1. ( ) Please, Rhonda, don't pay attention to the other kids.

2. ( ) My daughter always has good sense, even though she's a little rebellious at times.

3. ( ) When I work, I work hard.

4. ( ) There's no water, no grass, no trees for hundreds of miles.

5. ( ) Jim, can you come here for a minute?

6. ( ) The handkerchief, which bore my initials, was incriminating.

7. ( ) Gypsy, of his own accord, headed up the incline.

8. ( ) Dead cedar and pine trees lay everywhere, with their contorted limbs reaching out as if asking for sympathy.

9. ( ) In fact, I like my coffee that way.

10. ( ) My sister was born May 23, 1975, at 12:30 in the afternoon.

11. ( ) Upon my grandfather's grave, I've never been quite so terrified.

12. ( ) A long, low, steady rumble filled the air.

Semicolons

A **semicolon** (;) *is used to indicate a major division in a sentence and to eliminate confusion when commas are present.*

A semicolon is a combination of a comma and a period. It is used to indicate a greater pause than a comma; but, a weaker pause than a period.

Separating Independent Clauses

Use a semicolon between two main clauses that are closely related and are of equal rank. Do not use the semicolon to separate a clause from a phrase.

> It is true in peace; it is not true in war.
>
> Everybody was famished; everything was eaten.

Use a semicolon in place of a coordinating conjunction to join the parts of a compound sentence.

> I don't take my dogs for a walk; my dogs take me.
> (The conjunction left out could possibly have been *but.*)

Preceding Transitional, Connecting Words

Use a semicolon in compound sentences before transitional words (also known as conjunctive adverbs) such as: moreover, however, for example, therefore. Use a comma after the transitional word.

> I like skiing; moreover, I go every year.
>
> Time is running out; however, that fact doesn't seem to matter to you.

Preceding Explanatory Abbreviations

Semicolons are used before appositives, explanatory words, and abbreviations such as: i.e., e.g., namely, for example, or especially. Use a comma after the explanatory word or abbreviation.

> Fruitcakes contain sweet things; namely, candied fruit.
> The diary contained secrets; i.e., sneaking candy bars into her dorm room.

Exercise A.   Replace each conjunction with a semicolon.

1. Jackie is going to Oxford and Steven is going to Georgetown.
2. In old Westerns, cowboys with white hats were the good guys and cowboys with the black hats were the bad guys.
3. I received a *C* in Math but I received an *A* in Science.
4. Oak burns slowly but pine burns quickly.
5. Would you like French dressing or would you like bleu cheese?

Exercise B.   Place a semicolon between the two main clauses.

1. It's raining and pouring the old man's snoring.
2. The dog howled the cat meowed.
3. The sale begins at noon however, it's good to arrive early.
4. Ask me no questions I'll tell you no lies.
5. James loved Sarah furthermore, he wanted to marry her.

Avoiding Confusion with Commas

Semicolons are used to join clauses or phrases which also contain commas. In the sentence, *Jody is in the garden; Martin, in the field*, change the comma to the verb *is*. Now we have two main clauses of equal weight. *Jody is in the garden; Martin* **is** *in the field*.

Exercise C. Correctly place semicolons in the following sentences. Then, substitute a verb for the comma.

1. Oak burns slowly pine, quickly.
2. Time flies quickly when you're having fun life, slowly while you're young.
3. Snow White is lovely and innocent the wicked witch, vain and horrid.
4. The dance craze in the forties was the jitterbug the fifties the bop and the sixties the twist.
5. The sermon begins at 7:00 p.m. the social hour, at 8:30 p.m.
6. War is destructive peace, constructive.

Semicolons are used to join items in a series when a comma also appears. This avoids confusion about where to pause (i.e., I visited Amarillo, Texas; Flagstaff, Arizona; and Taos, New Mexico).

Exercise D. Place semicolons and commas correctly in the following sentences.

1. In Gramp's day, movies were 20 cents candy and chewing gum 5 cents sodas, 10 cents and a Marvel comic book 25 cents.
2. We'll discuss logging, conservation and recycling use of private forests for tree farming and endangered species.
3. Her eyes, bright and brown her fur, golden, shiny and soft showed me the care my horse had been given at the stables.
4. I stopped, aimed, fired the deer calmly looked at me, and fled.
5. Darrin was terrible at two unbearable at three but, extremely lovable at four.

Exercise E. Correctly place semicolons and commas in the following sentences.

1. We waited and waited for the bus to Woodstock it finally came three hours late.
2. Slowly the moon rose hugely it loomed.
3. Time is of the essence however haste makes waste.
4. Bright red coats gleamed weapons glinted gaunt wizened soldiers leaned forward on racy slender steeds.
5. There are three things I need from the store namely rice walnuts and celery.
6. The broken vase torn books and ripped curtains can never be replaced but the neighbors offer this gift to help ease your pain.
7. Many a time I have wished for riches many a time my wishes were granted.
8. The endangered rivers included the Klamath River Oregon the Salmon River Idaho the Eel River Northern California and the Colorado River Southern California.
9. Someone's in the kitchen with Dinah someone's in the kitchen I know.
10. Cake is a wonderful dessert especially, chocolate cake.

Colons

*The **colon** (:) formally introduces an elaboration, a summation, an explanation, or a quotation. The colon is also used to separate numbers.*

Formal Correspondence

After salutations.

    Dear Miss Jones:

    To Whom It May Concern:

After the abbreviation used for reference.

    RE: Invoice # 92712 dated 7/6/92

After abbreviations used below the signature line.

    cc: (carbon copy)

    Encl: (indicates enclosures sent with the original)

    SC:cgc (separates supervisor or originator of correspondence and the typist or preparer of the correspondence)

Appositive, Explanation, or Quotation

Appositive: I've wondered about John all along: whether he had graduated or not.

Explanation: "We hold these truths to be self-evident: that all men are created equal, ..."

                           —Thomas Jefferson, 1776

Quotation: Martin Luther King, Jr. quoted from the Declaration of Independence:

    "...that all men are created equal,..."

Separating Independent Clauses

When the second clause of two main clauses is an amplification of the first, separate the two clauses with a colon. The second clause generally begins with a capital letter; especially, with quotations.

> I saw the sign too late: Please stay off the grass.
> I quote from *Hamlet*: "To be or not to be, that is the question."

Introducing Lists or Items

The colon is used to preface more than one item of information. The colon itself is preceded in this situation by a *determining* word or phrase . Such determining words or phrases are *for example*, *the following*, *as stated*, *below*, or *as noted above*.

There is a catch, though. Never use a colon directly after a verb or directly after a preposition.

Correct: Please bring the following to the test room: a no. 2 pencil, an eraser, a calculator, and a slide rule.

Incorrect: The items to bring are: a no. 2 pencil, an eraser, a calculator, and a slide rule.

Between Titles and Subtitles

> *Maid Marian and Robin Hood: The Later Years*
> *Lassie: A Story About a Boy and His Dog*

Separating Groups of Numbers

Clock time

The colon symbol follows each portion of time. If you want to indicate that five hours, thirty minutes, and fifteen seconds have elapsed since midnight, you separate each portion of time with a colon, e.g., 5:30:15. (Usually we are only required to indicate the hours and minutes.)

Proportions

We use proportions in time, but also in mathematics and chemistry. For example, you must mix ingredients proportionately in cooking: Two parts water to one part flour equals 2:1.

Citations and References

The colon separates citations from religious passages, lines in poetry, and references from magazines.

Biblical reference: John 6:3:4 (Book of John, Chapter 6, Verse 3, Line 4)

Plays: *Othello* I:3:12 (Play of *Othello*, Act I, Scene 3, Line 12)

Journal reference: *Early Amer Life* XXVII(6): 50-9 (*Early American Life*, Volume 27, Issue 6, Pages 50 through 59)

Exercise A.   Insert colons wherever needed in the following sentences.

1. My favorite sports are baseball, volleyball, and soccer.
2. The following are foods I like hot dogs, chili beans, and cottage cheese.
3. The history lesson was about Columbus, settling of the Americas, and displacement of Indians.
4. We studied the following Columbus, the settling of the Americas, and the displacement of Indians.
5. Here are the chapters we need to study I, IV, and V.
6. It is said A bird in the hand is worth two in the bush.
7. Above the counter loomed the sign No shoes, no shirt, no service.

Exercise B.   Rewrite the following using colons to indicate a division.

1. Seven-thirty a.m.
2. Seventeen minutes after five o'clock
3. Twelve minutes and fifty-five seconds before midnight.
4. Use two parts flour to four parts water.
5. Read pages 23-30 of the third chapter of the first section.

Exercise C. Place semicolons and colons correctly in the following sentences.

1. I'd say "yes" to almost any food right now especially, hamburgers.
2. If you pass this test, you'll be a high ranker someone who'll be hired very soon.
3. This program is dedicated to children's entertainment face painting, juggling, and mime, to name a few.
4. We're interested in organizations involved in physical fitness activities i.e., health clubs, sports, gymnastics.
5. The Old Country Inn's opening-day ceremony offers the following specials two nights with room-service breakfast, $40.00 free dessert with dinner, first night and all-you-can-eat buffet, second night.

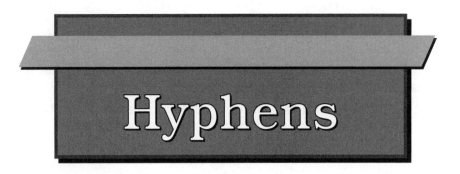

Hyphens

*A **hyphen(-)** links words and word parts.*

Joining Compound Nouns

commander-in-chief   merry-go-round

great-grandmother   stick-in-the-mud

president-elect

Joining Compound Adjectives before a Noun

a *bluish-green* car

the *chocolate-covered* almonds

a *community-sponsored* event

the *hurricane-force* winds

a *two-sided* issue

a *well-educated* person

a *well-known* celebrity

a *second-story* man

Sometimes short phrases are used as adjectives.

the *up-to-date* information   a *face-to-face* discussion

his *I-don't-care* attitude   a *run-of-the-mill* job

a *well-to-do* person   on a *first-come-first-served* basis

our *out-of-town* guests   a *how-to-do-it* course

the *older-than-twenty* set

The hyphen has a historical heritage as a fuser of words. A hyphen often links two words which, over time, become one word.

post-man   has become   *postman*

basket-ball   has become   *basketball*

Stringing words and phrases together by means of hyphens is not the polished manner of formal English, but the informality of casual speech or friendly banter.

Keep this in mind when you use the hyphen to join adjectives or nouns, or to create lengthier phrases.

Some words that are hyphenated today will become single words in the years to come.

Numbers and Fractions

Use a hyphen for the compound numbers twenty-one to ninety-nine.

sixty-six   forty-nine   eighty-three

Use a hyphen in fractions.

one-half   seven-ninths   three-fourths

Some writers choose not to hyphenate fractions used as nouns.

Three fourths of the eligible voters cast their ballots.

Use a hyphen to indicate a span between numerals.

1927-1932   pages 428-613

Use a hyphen in a series.

two-, three-, four-, and five-story buildings

Use a hyphen for compound adjectives having a numeral as a first element.

24-inch ruler   3-week vacation
5-to-4 vote

Special Cases to Join a Prefix to a Root Word

Use a hyphen to join a prefix to a proper noun or proper adjective.

all-American   post-World War I
pre-Columbian   anti-Mafia
pro-French
mid-Atlantic

Use a hyphen after a common prefix like ex-, self-, and all-.

> ex-convict
> self-righteous
> self-satisfied
> all-purpose

Use a hyphen to prevent an awkward letter combination or a misreading.

anti-inflammatory	un-uniform
semi-invalid	micro-organism
re-enter	

re-creation of events	:	recreation is healthy
re-count ballots	:	recount the chain-of-events
re-sign the check	:	resign from office
re-lay the carpet	:	relay the message

Special Cases to Join a Suffix to a Root Word

Use a hyphen to prevent an awkward letter combination or misreading.

> a bell-like ring
> Miami-like weather
> thrill-less

Letters of Spelled Words

Use a hyphen to indicate the spelling of a word.

> Revise that sentence by replacing t-h-e-r-e with t-h-e-i-r.

Syllabication

Use hyphens to divide syllables.

> re-serve
> lei-sure
> sea-son-a-ble
> mis-ap-pro-pri-ate
> ich-thy-ol-o-gy

The following are useful guidelines for hyphens and syllables in written text:

---

1. Hyphenate words between syllables.

2. Never divide a one-syllable word.

3. Never place a one-letter syllable at the beginning or end of a line.

    e-vade   i-tem   sleep-y

4. A two-letter word ending should not be carried over to a next line.

    cred-it   lay-er   sure-ly

5. Refrain from dividing proper nouns or proper adjectives.

    Toronto   Switzerland   Atlantic

6. Divide hyphenated words only at the hyphen.

    merry-go-round   mass-transportation   self-indulgent

Exercise A. Hyphenate any appropriate words and phrases.

1.	three year term	2.	a term of three years
3.	a comment off the record	4.	an off the record comment
5.	quiet spoken person	6.	a person who speaks quietly
7.	a hero who is known well	8.	a well known hero
9.	an accident prone person	10.	a person who is accident prone
11.	sister in law	12.	top coat
13.	automobile	14.	a write in candidate
15.	an exmayor	16.	a 7 to 6 vote
17.	one half cup	18.	biology
19.	a runon sentence	20.	a poverty stricken people
21.	40 hour week	22.	5 string banjo
23.	Uboat	24.	up to date license
25.	in the wind	26.	pre Civil War
27.	allied	28.	all inclusive
29.	a hillless landscape	30.	the right time of the day
31.	midship	32.	exculpate
33.	two story house	34.	unCanadian
35.	three eighths	36.	freight train
37.	thirty odd years old	38.	halfback
39.	half baked idea	40.	an A frame house

Exercise B. The following words are hyphenated and supposed to be words at the end of a line. Knowing this, why is the hyphenation incorrect or improper? (Refer to "Useful Guidelines" on the opposite page.)

1. a-lone
2. shor-ten
3. six-ty
4. Shake-spearean
5. o-boe

Exercise C. Provide any necessary hyphenation.

1. I'll recover the chair when I recover from the flu.
2. The baby was ill clothed for such cold weather.
3. Why would such a respected committee write such an off the wall report?
4. The graduates were 21 23 years old.
5. Stay tuned for up to the minute news.
6. The mill is hiring part time employees.
7. Alicia and Elena are coowners of the business.
8. How often have your parents had a heart to heart talk with you?
9. I received seventy five cents in change.
10. Please change this ten dollar bill into ten dollar bills.
11. Ex presidents are quickly forgotten.
12. It is a well known fact that two thirds of the money was lost.
13. Is a self made person self confident?
14. Please readdress this envelope.
15. His happiness was short lived, because what he thought was a well implemented plan was really an ill conceived one.
16. My favorite program was preempted by a fast breaking news event.
17. In our class eight, nine, and ten year old gymnasts are grouped together.
18. Is it time for your midafternoon nap?
19. He turned down a $50,000 a year salary.
20. We rented a 16 foot sailboat for a 3 week cruise.
21. The L shaped living room is two thirds the size of our family room.
22. Our son in law owns 10 15 different cars.
23. You can have a two, three, or four year lease.
24. The drop off slot is next to the self closing door.
25. Who is the prime minister elect?

Parentheses

Parentheses are used to set off parenthetical, supplementary, or illustrative information, as well as to enclose figures or letters used for enumeration within a sentence.

Parentheses are used, primarily, to set off extra information; as are commas and dashes. Commas are used for extra information that is closely related to the full sentence. Dashes are used for information that is more abrupt, more emphatic. (See the discussion of commas and dashes.)

Parentheses fall between commas and dashes in their relationship to the main part of the sentence. Use parentheses for material that is not intended to be an intrinsic part of the main sentence. The enclosed material could be considered incidental or digressive and could almost be dismissed by the reader.

Parenthetic, Supplementary, or Illustrative Information

A number of states (Oregon, for instance) have bottle bills.

Batman (our twenty-year-old cat) is a grey-and-white short hair.

After his very first book (1992), he was lauded as a major, new talent.

The citation (for excessive speed) was stiff.

The jacket cost too much ($49.95).

The story (see accompanying copy) is enough to make you wonder.

Our spokesperson (E. Giuditta Collins) did not arrive until Thursday evening.

The old crone (actually she was only forty) loved animals.

The information within parentheses can range from a short, pointed comment to a full sentence. A complete sentence within parentheses is not capitalized, and it does not need a period. But if the parentheses fall outside a sentence, the first word of the sentence must be capitalized and the sentence must contain an ending mark within the closing parenthesis.

My great-grandfather left for North America (his boat departed from Genoa, Italy) in 1854.

The class has attracted many students. (Students come from many backgrounds.)

Enclosing Figures or Letters Used as Enumeration within a Sentence

Use these steps to assemble the cards: (1) sort, (2) collate, (3) cut, and (4) place in the box.

The survey asked (a) how old I was, (b) my occupation, and (c) my party affiliation.

Punctuation and Parentheses

1. Place a question mark or an exclamation point inside parentheses if it is part of the parenthetical information. If it is not, place a question mark or exclamation point outside.

2. Always place commas, semicolons, or colons after a closing parenthesis.

Exercise A. Provide necessary parentheses.

1. I nearly called my accountants Carter and Carter.

2. Complete this form the one marked 1040A, and return it to this office.

3. Our committee has several objectives: a increase revenues, b increase membership, and c provide community service.

4. Please find an enclosed check for ten dollars $10.

5. His call was prompt within five minutes.

6. Parentheses are used to enclose 1 certain words, 2 certain phrases, and 3 numbers and letters.

7. In 1993, the Oregon Trail was marked with a sesquicentennial 150th celebration.

8. He called last week was it Friday?, but I was not here.

9. We can see a great change by comparing our income before 1980 first chart with our income after 1980 second chart.

10. (Punctuate a separate sentence.) She did not try to answer. She could not.

Dashes

*A **dash** is a sudden break separating parts of a sentence to denote emphasis.*

A dash is indicated by two hyphens on a typewriter (--). For handwriting, a dash is an unbroken line the length of two hyphens. In typesetting and desktop computing, an em dash (—) serves as a dash (an em dash is about the width of the capital letter M). No space precedes or follows a dash.

Parenthetic Information

You will recall that parenthetic information includes words, sentences, or phrases that are inserted into sentences to provide supplemental information or explanation, or to add illustration. Parenthetic information can be set off by commas, parentheses, or dashes.

Writers use the appropriate punctuation to underscore their intended emphasis. Commas are the mildest separator of parenthetic information. They leave the comments they enclose closely connected with the remaining portion of the sentence. Parentheses minimize the connection of the parenthetic information they enclose with the remaining portion of the sentence. By contrast, dashes are meant to set off parenthetic information sharply. All three punctuation marks are used for emphasis.

The difference between commas, parentheses, and dashes may be lost on the casual reader. But to the writer who is trying to distinguish his or her narrative or text, the use of commas, parentheses, and dashes in parenthetic positions is very clear.

> The town—as many critics have stated—is noisy, polluted, and in decay.
>
> My father met J. Fred Willard—the renowned courthouse reporter— at an antique auto show.
>
> It was plain—could there be any question?— that he was ill-prepared for the examination.
>
> Three competing companies—A.W. Morris, Fuentes Brothers, and Goldman, Ltd.— vied for the contract.
>
> The clerk—shall we call him a knave or a fool?— sold the tickets for one-half the actual price of the product.
>
> Several of my closest friends—Marsha, Elise, and Emily—refused to attend the celebration.

The use of the dash in the last example prevents confusion. The use of commas is apt to confuse the reader:

> Several of my closest friends, Marsha, Elise, and Emily, refused to attend the celebration.

Hesitation or Incomplete Thought

The dash is used in dialogue to denote breathlessness or confused thought.

> "Wait—I—no, let's turn here."
> "You're—you're not going to do that!" he exclaimed.

After a Series to Set Off a Summary

> Relish, mustard, sauerkraut, onions—I like my hot dog loaded.
> Biology 207, Chemistry 200, upper level math—all these are required for graduation.
> Some of my closest friends—for example, Marsha, Elise, and Emily—refused to attend the celebration.

Short, Terse Emphasis

> We are all alike—on the outside.
>   —Mark Twain
>
> The zealots have only one goal—money.
>
> Right now—at this very instant—you could be the Grand Prize winner.

The level of emphasis for a word or phrase is often a subjective one. The above examples could be written using commas in place of the dashes. But dashes were used by the authors to weight their words.

Combine Figures, Capital Letters, or Figures and Capital Letters

> Exhibit 5—C
> DC—3 (airplane)
> I—5 (interstate highway)
> ABC—TV Network
> KOPB—AM—FM—TV
> 301–342–5734 (area code and phone number)

After a Quotation to Set-off the Source

We are all alike—on the outside.

—Mark Twain

Exercise A. Here are six Mark Twain quotations. They all use a dash—one uses five dashes. Place the dashes as Mark Twain did.

1. Tomorrow night I appear for the first time before a Boston audience 4000 critics.

   —Letter to to Pamela Clemens Moffit

2. Put all your eggs in the one basket and WATCH THAT BASKET.
   —*Pudd'nhead Wilson*

3. Each person is born to one possession which outvalues all his others his last breath.
   —*Pudd'nhead Wilson*

4. Biographies are but the clothes and buttons of the man the biography of the man himself cannot be written.
   —*Autobiography*

5. Adam was but human this explains it all. He did not want the apple for the apple's sake, he wanted it only because it was forbidden.
   —*Pudd'nhead Wilson*

6. I do not want Michael Angelo for breakfast for lunch for dinner for tea for supper or between meals.
   —*Innocents Abroad*

Exercise B. Here are three more quotations. Place the dashes as the author did. Place dashes to denote the source.

1. Yesterday, December 7, 1941 a day which will live in infamy the United States of America was suddenly and deliberately attacked. . . .

   Franklin D. Roosevelt, War Message to Congress

2. There is only one success to be able to spend your life in your own way.

   Christopher Morley, *Where the Blue Begins*

3. I don't think necessity is the mother of invention invention, in my opinion, arises directly from idleness, possibly also from laziness.

   Agatha Christie, *An Autobiography*

Exercise C. Use the dash correctly in each sentence.

1. Public officials should act responsibly not like bumbling fools.

2. Your clothes should be washed the laundromat is open until midnight and ironed.

3. "Funny thing" he said, never completing his thought.

4. Tall timber, lush undergrowth, and abundant water these things impress a first-time visitor to western Oregon.

5. After years of training, she achieved her goal the chief executive officer of a large corporation.

6. I suppose you agree KOAP AM FM is an excellent public radio station.

7. Calculus, differential equations, statistics my hardest courses are all math.

8. "Watch watch out! The ladder is fall!"

9. I will never never I say never return to such an unfriendly business.

10. She was playing I remember it well with a friend in the rain.

NO. 2

Mid-Review Test

Punctuate the following exercises correctly—using the techniques you've learned to this point.

Exercise A.

> January 15 1992
>
> Jack Jones Jr
> 1122 Miramar Dr #2
> Santa Clara Calif
>
> Dear Jack
>
> I m planning a going away party Sept 17 for Miss Stevens who is joining the Peace Corps. Please let me know if you can attend and Ill make preparations. By the way could you lend me your copy of American History Illustrated Vol 27 Number 6? Theres an article on Julia Ward Howe the author of the Battle Hymn of the Republic that Id like to read.
>
> Thanks
>
> Jean

Exercise B.

1. Governor Johnson a Democrat and family practitioner supports the bill that bans smoking in a variety of locations from video arcades to airport waiting rooms.

2. The Military Park Hotel see the before and after photos in your program in Newark New Jersey was demolished by an implosion.

Exercise C. In addition to punctuating the following correctly, write out the full word(s) for abbreviations.

> This years fundraiser to raise money to fight M.S. will be held at mt hood meadows. There will be volunteers at the site accepting apps for coaches for the Manitoba quad a baseball team.

Brackets

Brackets are used to supplement or connect information.

Editorial Comments, Corrections, and Interpolations

Brackets are the only punctuation mark that can make it clear that enclosed material is not part of a quotation.

One standard editorial comment is the use of [*sic*], informing the reader that an error appears in an original passage.

> The mayor wrote, "I have many fiends [*sic*] in high places."

Or an editor may supply the correctly spelled word in brackets.

> The mayor wrote, "I have many fiends [friends] in high places."

An editor may supply information.

> "In that year [1879], we left St. Louis for San Francisco."

An editor may accent part of a passage.

> "The debt has *not* been satisfied." [Emphasis added]

An editor may add material when quoted text is unclear, incomplete, or omits words or punctuation.

> In his Majesty['s] service—in this ship indeed—there are Englishmen forced to fight for the King against their will.
> —Herman Melville, *Billy Budd*

Parentheses Within Parentheses

Mark Twain (the pseudonym [penname] of Samuel Clemens) is known for *The Adventures of Huckleberry Finn*.

Government agencies (such as the Federal Bureau of Investigation [FBI]) must be held responsible for their conduct.

Exercise A. Place brackets and parentheses appropriately.

1. He said, "Boots and Max both Manx cats were found in our neighbor's backyard."

2. He says Boots and Max both Manx cats were found in our neighbor's backyard.

3. My brother the youngest of six children is responsible for all morning chores.

4. The article told about life in "Phenix, Arizona sic," and "Memphis, Tenesee sic."

5. The sheriff Gorge Diaz has been elected to office seven times.

6. "The sheriff Gorge Diaz has been elected to office seven times."

7. ". . . ask what *you* can do for your country." Emphasis added.

8. "In that year 1922, we had lived in Ontario and New York," his diary recorded.

9. "I will disperse a check for seven hundred dollars $700 as quickly as possible."

10. "The act was a feet *sic* of dexterity and skill," the reviewer wrote.

Ellipses

Ellipses (. . .) indicate omissions from quoted material.

Beginning of a Quoted Passage

"No man is an island, entire of itself; every man is a piece of the continent, a part of the main. If a clod be washed away by the sea, Europe is the less, as well as if a promontory were, as well as if a manor of thy friend's or of thine own were. Any man's death diminishes me because I am involved in mankind, and therefore never send to know for whom the bell tolls; it tolls for thee."

—John Donne

Generally, it is not necessary to use an ellipsis at the beginning of a selected passage of any length. An exception might be the desire of a writer to indicate that quoted material preceded the excerpt used.

For instance, from above, quoting from the second sentence:

". . . If a clod be washed away by the sea, . . ."

The writer might use the ellipsis at the beginning of the quote to indicate that the passage began before, "If a clod . . . ."

Noting this exception as a choice of personal style, points of ellipsis are generally not used to begin a quoted passage.

Middle of a Quoted Passage

"No man is an island . . . every man is a piece of the continent, a part of the main. . . ."

The first ellipsis uses three dots (. . .). This indicates omission from within a single sentence.

An ellipsis plus a period (. . . .) are used in the middle of quoted passages when there is an omission to the end of a sentence, the beginning of a succeeding sentence, or one or more complete sentences.

"No man is an island . . . every man is a piece of the continent, a part of the main. . . . Any man's death diminishes me because I am involved in man-kind."

As indicated by "main. . . . Any," a complete sentence is omitted between *main* and *Any*.

End of a Quoted Passage

"No man is an island. . . ."

The sentence has been cut short. The period plus the ellipsis are used because what remains of the sentence is grammatically complete.

A writer may argue that omitting the period ("No man is an island . . .") would indicate the sentence is not fully quoted.

Exercise A. Lincoln's Gettysburg Address. If the material within the brackets was eliminated, which points of ellipsis would be used to indicate the omission (. . . or . . . .)?

"Four score and seven years ago our fathers brought forth on this continent a new nation, conceived in liberty and dedicated to the proposition that all men are created equal.

"Now we are engaged in a great civil war[, testing whether that nation, or any nation so conceived and so dedicated, can long endure.] We are met on a great battle field of that war. We have come to dedicate [a portion of] that field as a final resting-place for those who here gave their lives [that that nation might live.] It is altogether fitting and proper that we should do this.

"But, in a larger sense, we cannot dedicate [– we cannot consecrate—we cannot hallow –] this ground. The brave men, living and dead, who struggled here, have consecrated it far above our poor power to add or detract. The world [will little not, nor long remember what we say here, but it] can never forget what they did here. It is for us the living, rather, to be dedicated here to the unfinished work which they who fought here have thus far so nobly advanced.

"It is rather for us to [be here dedicated to the great task remaining before us—that from these honored dead we take increased devotion to that cause for which they gave the last full measure of devotion; that we here highly] resolve that these dead shall not have died in vain; that this nation, under God, shall have a new birth of freedom, and that government of the people, by the people, for the people, shall not perish from the earth."

Slashes

*The **slash** (/)* is used to divide lines of quoted poetry, to separate equally applied terms, and to indicate numeric fractions.*

Separating Terms that Are Equally Applicable

Critics often describe her as a playwright/poet.

Don't confuse use of the slash with use of the hyphen. The slash pairs two terms (usually nouns) of equal weight, whereas the hyphen actually joins two words into one.

The appearance of the slash is recent. Its use is rarely acceptable in formal English. The effect of the slash in speech and in casual writing could easily be chided as a lazy manner of expression.

Indicating Numeric Fractions

She hurled the discus 127 feet 9-1/2 inches.

The slash for fractions is well suited for typewriters and computers.

* The slash is also referred to as a virgule (poetry) or a solidus (mathematics).

Final
Assessment Test

Exercise A.   Identify the following abbreviations.

1. msg.
2. R.S.V.P.
3. R.I.P.
4. B.C.
5. Blvd.

6. Apr.
7. A.P.R.
8. M.D.
9. M.A.S.H.
10. rpt.

Exercise B.   Insert capitals, commas, apostrophes, and quotation marks where needed.

1. Shell be comin round the mountain, is a song about a woman wagon master.
2. When I start to argue, my father always says: No ifs, ands, or buts about it.
3. Its just your opinion, isnt it? Emily queried.
4. Dont eat Dads donut!
5. The brothers did each others chores.

Exercise C.   Capitalize, punctuate, use parentheses, and italicize (underline), as needed.

1. kids will be entertained this sunday during the 8th annual asian celebration being held at the lane county fairgrounds. the official opening will begin with a colorful chinese lion. japanese drumming by eugene city taiko a local troupe will follow.

2. In an extraordinary collaboration by detroits automakers, general motors, ford, and chrysler are discussing building jointly an electric car therefore meeting the requirements of the clean air law first enacted in california.

3. Dear Mr Johnson

    I'll be your big brother at Mt Loyola College which you plan to attend in the fall The following items may be useful a tape recorder a lap top computer and a printer. Please be at Allen Hall at 9 30 a m sharp The lecture will center around an article in Global Science magazine aka GSM vol 253(1) 45 52 1989 The title is The Manatee Its Habitat and Habits Remember promptness is not only important to the lecturer it is also important to you.

    Sincerely John Tubbs

4. the weather service office in new york city put the storm's size in perspective By the time snow was expected to start in the city around dawn saturday the center of the storm would still be over western ontario some 700 miles away.

Exercise D. Correct any punctuation, capitalization, or reference to numbers as needed.

1. 12 people purchased tickets to the lecture entitled travels through europe.
2. I have better than average grades this semester.
3. He is a member of the united auto workers UAW.
4. Elena my younger daughter enters school next year.
5. These party favors they cost less than a dollar are available at the card shop.

Answers

Note: (<u>Underlining</u> and *italics* are interchangeable)

Beginning Assessment Test
Page 1-2

A. Abbreviations.
1. Mrs.
2. Dr.
3. Atty.
4. volt
5. Av. or Ave.
6. Sun.
7. Mo./MO
8. A.D.
9. E.S.T.
10. ft.

B. Apostrophes.
1. I'm a little teapot, short and stout.
2. How many *T*'s are there in this sentence?
3. This is Mary's address. I don't know her sister's address.
4. The women's movement in the '60s was part of the campaign for Civil Rights.
5. The movie, *Summer of '42*, took place during the United States' involvement in WWII.

C. Capitalization.
1. February is Black History month. Throughout this month, we will publish interesting moments from the history of black people in Oregon. You can read about these fascinating histories every Monday and Wednesday on the front page of our City/Region section.
2. While Minnesota struggles through another losing season, Doug West has emerged as one of the best young shooting guards in the NBA.
3. Come to Taco Bell for a special "Cinco de Mayo" treat. Your hostess will be Senorita Donna Green.

D. Identify symbols.
1. colon
2. parentheses
3. dashes
4. slash
5. semicolon
6. hyphen
7. quotation marks
8. brackets

E. Commas, Semicolons, and Colons.
1. Then she slowly sank down, laid back her ears, bared her teeth, and hissed; at the same time, throwing both paws out viciously. Kitty may have rested; however, she did not sleep. Hours after I had crawled into my sleeping bag, in the silence of night, I heard her working to get free. I heard the clink of her chain, the crack of her teeth, the scrape of her claws. How tireless she was.

F. Italics and Quotation Marks.
1. She said, "Be sure to dot your *i*'s and cross your *t*'s."
2. One of my favorite short stories is "Big Two-Hearted River" from the book, *In Our Time.*
3. Have you seen the production of *Phantom of the Opera*?
4. I listen each afternoon to "All Things Considered" on the radio.
5. "Do you recall," she asked, "the address?"

G. Parentheses and Brackets.
1. The book, printed nearly a century ago (1894), is valuable.
2. The letter was dated "April 31, 1092 [sic]" and signed by my father.
3. Andrew Jackson ("Old Hickory") served as the seventh president (1829-1837).
4. "The society, Redwood Protectors (RP), was established in 1922."
5. The instructions read as follows: (1) remove the top, (2) locate the bulb, and (3) replace the fuse.

H. Numbers.
1. 1 dog, 1 cat, 3 mice
2. seven o'clock
3. a bargain at $4.95
4. Act III, Scene VI, line 52
5. 62%

I. Hyphens.

1. a 6-to-2 vote
2. ex-mayor
3. hot-dog buns
4. OK
5. anti-communist
6. thirty-three
7. all-out manhunt
8. OK
9. three-quarters of an inch
10. mother-in-law

J. Dashes.

1. Lettuce, tomato, cheese—everything on my hamburger, please.
2. It was obvious—who would object—that the award was deserved.
3. I like this version—"interpretation," if you will—of the song.

Abbreviations

Page 4
Exercise A.

1. Mrs. Collins
2. Hon. Allen Baker, Jr.
3. Mlle. et Mme. Jordache
4. Dr. John D. Smith or John D. Smith, M.D.
5. Rev. Dobbs
6. Richard Browning, D.D.S. or Dr. Richard Browning
7. Ms. Mary Louise Simpson, CEO
8. Sra. Cabrillo
9. Maj. Gen. Koop, Ret.
10. Ste. Joan of Arc

Page 6
Exercise B.

1. Young Men's Christian Association
2. United Nations
3. United States of America
4. United Nations International Children's Emergency Fund
5. Union of Soviet Socialist Republics
6. Daughters of the American Revolution
7. runs batted in
8. Automobile Association of America
9. rest and relaxation
10. Palestine Liberation Organization
11. Health Maintenance Organization
12. Central Intelligence Agency
13. Registered Nurse
14. I owe you
15. National Broadcasting Corporation

Exercise C.

1. I led the fund raiser in our town for **M.S.**
2. We danced at the **VFW** hall.
3. My friend's father was an **M.I.A.** soldier in Viet Nam.
4. **T.G.I.F.!**
5. I read Leon Uris' book **QB VII** twice.
6. The EEC includes France.
7. Did you know that **MSG** is a preservative for foods?
8. There were many programs on **TV** last month about **UFO**'s.
9. My brother was never **AWOL** while in the Navy.
10. Where is the **c.g.** on this aircraft.
11. Lonnie's psychology term paper is about **ESP.**
12. What is Babe Ruth's lifetime **rbi.**
13. I prefer news on **NPR** to news from **CBS.**
14. All radio stations are licensed by the **FCC.**
15. What is your **ZIP** code?

Page 8
Exercise D.

1. Answers will vary.
2. Answers will vary.

Page 10
Exercise E.

1. Dear Monica, Wait for me **at school** in the hallway next to Mr. Frasier's **room.** I need to go over the **assignment** for **questions** on the **examination** to be held on **Tuesday.** Also, **regarding Saturday** night: I have **included** Betty and Joan in the plans. Will you be wearing your blue dress, blue heels, blue earrings, **et cetera**? Well, I **must** run. I have an **appointment at** the dentist in twenty **minutes.** Yours truly, **Rebecca.**
2. **Colonel** John Jones, **retired,** ...state of **Alabama** last **month** to meet his **brother** for the **first** time in **seventeen years.**
3. Barbara Adams, **Attorney** at Law, sent **messages** to the **attention** of all **chief executive officers** in **charge** of telecommunications.
4. What is the **latitude** of **Northern California.**
5. That **company** packs tomatoes.
6. Eugene, **Oregon, United States of America,** is in Lane **County.**
7. I work on the **ninth floor** of the **federal building** on State **Street.**

8. The **Young Women's Christian Association** is located next to Beans **and** Franks **Delicatessen.**
9. On **Saturday morning,** a storm swept across towns from New York City to Atlanta, **Georgia.**
10. The storm moved east at **fifty miles per hour** and dumped **five feet** of snow in the **mountains.**

Apostrophes

Page 11
Exercise A.
1. "Shore, lady, **Yaqui's goin'** home," replied Ladd gently. **"An' considerin'** our troubles, I reckon we ought to thank God he knows the way."
2. My **name's** Belding. **I'm** the inspector and **I'd** like to know what you mean by taking up [all] my **rangers'** land claims.

Page 13
Exercise B.
1. I've (O) goat's (P)
2. Martina's (O) Teddy Bears' (P)
3. You're (O)
4. puppies' (P) waggin' (O)
5. Somebody's (O)

Page 14
Exercise C.

Singular	Plural
child	children
dog	dogs
vest	vests
mother	mothers
sheep	sheep
campus	campuses
folly	follies
island	islands
woman	women
caress	caresses
justice	justices
fox	foxes
bush	bushes
father-in-law	fathers-in-law
person	persons/people

Singular Possessive	Plural Possessive
child's	children's
dog's	dogs'
vest's	vests'
mother's	mothers'

sheep's	sheep's
campus'	campuses'
folly's	follies'
island's	islands'
woman's	women's
caress's	caresses'
justice's	justices'
fox's	foxes'
bush's	bushes'
father-in-law's	fathers-in-law's
person's	people's

Page 15
Exercise D.
1. The Mexicans were hastily erecting adobe houses upon **Ladd's** 160 acres, upon Dick **Gale's,** upon Jim **Lash's** and **Thorne's.**
2. The mid-Atlantic and Northeast coastline was especially susceptible to the powerful **Nor'easter** which blew in last December.
3. **It'll** be an easy climb to the **mountain's** crest, but it will become difficult as you near the **eagle's** nest.
4. Sunday is reserved for a trip to **Grandma's** house.
5. The only cars at the beginning of the century were Model **A's** and Model **T's.**

Exercise E.
1. **"It's** a fine day today," said Betty.
2. **That's** a mighty fine horse **you've** purchased.
3. **I'd** bring my blue purse, but **its** clasp is broken.
4. **Apples** and **oranges:** they're all the same.
5. **"Somethin'** is wrong at the Applegate Farm," croaked Zeke.
6. **Susan's** attending her **brother's** farewell party.
7. Grandma always says, "Mind your **P's** and **Q's!"**
8. I said that **nobody's** going to find **your** mistake.
9. The **puppies'** and **kittens'** toys were lost in the fire.
10. **I'm** an ol' cowhand from the Rio Grande.

Capitalization

Page 17
Exercise A.
1. Answers will vary.
2. Answers will vary.
3. Answers will vary.

Page 19
Exercise B.
1. **A** tiny fuzzy bird peeked out of the nest.
2. **The** door opened slowly and **Bob** shouted, **"Boo!"**
3. **Let's** put this problem in perspective: **One** apple and one apple equal how many apples?
4. **Flooding** was severe along the **Atlantic** coast.
5. **Traffic** was snarled in the eastern and western parts of the state, and in the **South**.

Exercise C.
In an extraordinary collaboration by **Detroit's** automakers, **General Motors, Ford** and **Chrysler** are discussing building jointly an electric car to meet the requirements of the clean-air law first enacted in **California**, and recently adopted by several northeastern states.

Italics

Page 21-22
Exercise A.
1. Native New Englanders add an *r* to words ending in *a* and omit the *r* in words ending in *r*. For example, *sofa* sounds like *sofer* and *roller* sounds like *rolla*.
2. Would you rather listen to Mozart's *Eine Kleine Nachtmusik* or *Magic Flute*?
3. I recently read Shakespeare's comedy *All's Well that Ends Well* and his tragedy *Troilus and Cressida*.
4. Justice Goldberg delivered the opinion of the court in *Cox v. Louisiana*.
5. How many *s*'s are there in the word *Mississippi*?
6. The American Firefly (*Photinus pyralis*) is largely found east of the Mississippi River.
7. The words *bourgeois* and *milieu* have French origins.

8. *National Geographic, Smithsonian, Newsweek, Science, New Yorker*, and *Reader's Digest* arrive in the mail each month, and I read them all.
9. They worked as if they had been given *carte blanche* to change the world.
10. How many times have you seen *Star Wars* or *ET*?
11. Underline every *7* on the page.
12. The opposition successfully staged a *coup d' état* only to be overthrown six months later.
13. *Voyager* sent back exceptional photographs as it passed the planet Neptune.
14. Lindbergh's flight across the Atlantic in the *Spirit of St. Louis* took over thirty-three hours.
15. His words are a *non sequitur* to his actions.
16. Facetious contains the vowels *a, e, i, o,* and *u*.
17. The recent production of *The Marriage of Figaro* received a glorious review in the magazine *Opera Monthly*.
18. Many novels of intrigue are set on the *Orient Express*.
19. Have you read Cooper's *The Deerslayer* or *The Last of the Mochicans*?
20. Monday through Friday, we listen to *Morning Edition*. Saturday and Sunday, we listen to *Weekend Edition*.

Quotation Marks

Page 25
Exercise A.
1. *The Complete Short Stories of Mark Twain* (a book)
2. "Jabberwocky" (poem)
3. *The Saturday Evening Post* (magazine)
4. *A Prairie Home Companion* (radio program)
5. H.M.S. *Bounty* (ship)
6. "Lose Weight and Grow Young" (tabloid article)
7. "The News from Lake Woebegon" (segment of a radio program)
8. "The Economy and Employment Today" (an address)
9. *Oklahoma, Carousel, South Pacific* (musical productions)
10. "An Essay on Thrift" (essay)
11. *Raiders of the Lost Ark* (movie)
12. *Cleveland Plain Dealer* (newspaper)
13. "Modern Life" (magazine section)

14. *Das Rheingold* (musical work)
15. *Three Musicians* (painting)
16. "The Lottery" (short story)
17. "Singing in the Rain" (song)
18. *China Clipper* (aircraft)
19. "Saving: The Road to Prosperity" (journal article)
20. "The Last Decision" (book chapter)

Page 26
Exercise B.

1. **"Passage to India"** is a Walt Whitman poem from *Leaves of Grass*, while *A Passage to India* is a novel by E.M. Forster.
2. Charles Dickens' **"A Christmas Carol"** is a classic short story revisited every Christmas.
3. *In Our Time*, published in 1925, contains the venerable short stories: **"A Very Short Story," "Cat in the Rain," "My Old Man," "Indian Camp,"** and **"Out of Season."**
4. Albert Busby's article **"The Bees that Swarmed Los Angeles"** is a simple article on *Apis Mellifera*, the common honey bee.
5. An editorial in the *Register Guard* entitled **"Will Our Public Fund Education"** challenged taxpayers to invest in the future.

Exercise C

1. "Completion is impossible," said the supervisor, "before the first of next week."
2. "Is completion possible before next month?" asked the supervisor.
3. The so-called "valuable gift" was nothing short of worthless.
4. Don't confuse "allusion" with "illusion" in your speech or writing.
5. "Look out–look out for—," he stammered.
6. Telling a performer to "break a leg" is supposed to bring them good luck.
7. Your friend gives new meaning to the term "space cookie."
8. Stop humming "Three Blind Mice"!
9. "Go!" shouted the official.
10. My dictionary defines ennui as "boredom."
11. My brother faultered, "Why–why did you say that?"
12. "Follow me," she whispered, "and do as I do."

13. "A large crowd is expected," said the conductor.
14. The conductor said, "A large crowd is expected."
15. "A large crowd," said the conductor, "is expected."

Exercise D.
Answers will vary.

Numbers

Page 29
Exercise A.

1. The **two** letters were mailed June 23.
2. The IRS will receive well over **two million** (or **2 million**) tax returns per day during April.
3. The buffet can serve **fifty** people an hour.
4. The **tenth** annual meeting falls on Saturday.
5. **One hundred twenty-seven** people walked, 114 drove, and forty rode their bicycles.
6. A two-thirds majority is required.
7. She has a **2.5** grade point average.
8. Chapter **6**, exercise **2** is difficult.
9. We have two pigs, three cows, and forty-two chickens.
10. The purchase order required 32 **twelve-inch** rulers.
11. Make the check for **$2,648.00**.
12. The sales tax is **$1.49**.
13. Do you watch Channel **12** news at six o'clock.
14. The loan was for **6-1/2** percent (or **6-1/2%**).
15. The temperature dropped to **32°** Fahrenheit.
16. They sell packets of **twelve 3-1/8 inch** gaskets.
17. We arrived June **4th**, 1992.
18. Put it in the **2-3/4 by 6-1/2** inch book.
19. We were paid **$3.75** an hour.
20. The national debt is a mere **400** billion dollars.
21. Is your birthday on the **twenty-first** or **twenty-second** of November?
22. The game ended in a **6-to-3** Blue Jay victory.
23. Our appointment was for **2:30** p.m.
24. The supply made twenty-five **1/4** pound patties.
25. Elena has **seven** siblings ranging in age from **sixteen** to **thirty**.

Mid-Review Test, No.1

Page 30
Exercise A.
1. *exempli gratia* (for example)
2. National Broadcasting Corporation
3. Attorney
4. Department of Motor Vehicles
5. extra-sensory perception

Exercise B.
1. **Mr.** Jones will speak at the assembly tomorrow.
2. Janet Byers, **M.D.**, at **Ste.** Agnes Hospital, will take **Dr.** Monroe's calls today.
3. **Gen.** John Thomas Masters, **III, Ret.**
4. It is my pleasure to accept the invitation to **Sra.** del Mundo's party.
5. The sign on my father's door says Bradford L. Boynton, **Sr., Esq., LL.D.**

Exercise C.
1. Thomas **Jefferson** wrote the **Declaration** of **Independence** in 1776. **He** later was elected governor of **Virginia** and the third president of the **United States. He** designed **Monticello, his** unique home pictured on the nickel.
2. Scientists won't know how much information was collected until **Discovery** returns **Spartan** to **Earth. The** eight-day atmospheric research mission is scheduled to end **Friday** with a landing at **Kennedy Space Center.** Early **Tuesday** evening, astronauts videotaped the **Russian** space station **MIR** as the two spacecraft passed within 350 miles of one another.

Exercise D.
1. *My Fair Lady* is the musical version, "rendition," if you will, of George Bernard Shaw's *Pygmalion.*
2. The word, *holocaust,* comes from the Greek word which means "whole-burnt."
3. Ex-President Jimmy Carter's full name is "James Earl Carter."

Commas

Page 32
Exercise A.
1. (a) Thank you for <u>your kind thoughts, your gifts, and your prayers</u>.
2. (d) It was a <u>dark, stormy, and windy</u> night.
3. (e)Your doll is either <u>on the stereo, in your tool box, or under the bed.</u>
4. (b) Candy <u>ran, jumped, and dived</u> into the pool.
5. (a) I saw <u>Jeff, Amy, Dee, Jean, and Cam</u> at the conference.
6. (g) The kitten was a little fluffy ball of fur.
7. (f)I want to know <u>what I did, what I said, or what I forgot</u> that made her so mad at me.
8. (c) The child's forehead felt <u>hot, sticky, and feverish.</u>
9. (f)Let me know <u>which direction to take, how many miles I'll be traveling,</u> and <u>how long it should take me to get there.</u>
10. (b) Doug <u>read</u> the newspaper, <u>drank</u> a cup of decaf, <u>and drove</u> to work.

Page 34
Exercise B.
1. Notwithstanding Thomas's belief, which Doris shared, Andrea did not appear at all during the appointed hour.
2. When Sam and his friends went outside, Fido, his dog, was eating under the porch where he always stayed.
3. The storm was gathering on the anniversary of one of the worst storms on record, the Blizzard of 1888.
4. Jane, could you hand me the wrench— the one closest to the rear tire?
5. On August 6, 1945, the U.S. dropped the A-bomb on Hiroshima, Japan.
6. Doug prefers to go rafting, not to go hiking.
7. On the other hand, I think I'll go rafting, too.
8. Commas used correctly avoid confusion. **(none)**
9. FEMA and the American Red Cross activated emergency plans, including the Emergency Broadcast System.
10. In southern Louisiana, where it rarely snows, two inches of snow fell last night.

Exercise C.
1. (b) Please, Rhonda, don't pay attention to the other kids.
2. (c) My daughter always has good sense, even though she's a little rebellious at times.
3. (e) When I work, I work hard.
4. (a) There's no water, no grass, no trees for hundreds of miles.
5. (b) Jim, can you come here for a minute?
6. (d) The handkerchief, which bore my initials, was incriminating.
7. (c) Gypsy, of his own accord, headed up the incline.
8. (d) Dead cedar and pine trees lay everywhere, with their contorted limbs reaching out as if asking for sympathy.
9. (c) In fact, I like my coffee that way.
10. (f) My sister was born May 23, 1975, at 12:30 in the afternoon.
11. (e) Upon my grandfather's grave, I've never been quite so terrified.
12. (a) A long, low, steady rumble filled the air.

Semicolon

Page 36
Exercise A.
1. Jackie is going to Oxford; Steven is going to Georgetown.
2. In old Westerns, cowboys with white hats were the good guys; cowboys with the black hats were the bad guys.
3. I received a *C* in Math; I received an *A* in Science.
4. Oak burns slowly; pine burns quickly.
5. Would you like French dressing; would you like bleu cheese?

Exercise B.
1. It's raining and pouring; the old man's snoring.
2. The dog howled; the cat meowed.
3. The sale begins at noon; however, it's good to arrive early.
4. Ask me no questions; I'll tell you no lies.
5. James loved Sarah; furthermore, he wanted to marry her.

Exercise C.
1. Oak burns slowly; pine **burns** quickly.
2. Time flies quickly when you're having fun; life **moves** slowly while you're young.

3. Snow White is lovely and innocent; the wicked witch **is** vain and horrid.
4. The dance craze of the forties was the jitterbug; the fifties **was** the bop; and the sixties **was** the twist.
5. The sermon begins at 7:00 p.m.; the social hour **begins** at 8:30 p.m.
6. War is destructive; peace **is** constructive.

Page 37
Exercise D.
1. In Gramp's day, movies were 20 cents; candy and chewing gum, 5 cents; sodas, 10 cents; and a Marvel comic book, 25 cents.
2. We'll discuss logging, conservation and recycling; use of private forests for tree farming; and endangered species.
3. Her eyes, bright and brown; her fur, golden, shiny and soft; showed me the care my horse had been given at the stables.
4. I stopped, aimed, fired; the deer calmly looked at me, and fled.
5. Darrin was terrible at two; unbearable at three; but, extremely lovable at four.

Exercise E.
1. We waited and waited for the bus to Woodstock; it finally came three hours late.
2. Slowly the moon rose; hugely, it loomed.
3. Time is of the essence; however, haste makes waste.
4. Bright red coats gleamed; weapons glinted; gaunt, wizened soldiers leaned forward on racy, slender steeds.
5. There are three things I need from the store; namely, rice, walnuts, and celery.
6. The broken vase, torn books, and ripped curtains can never be replaced; but the neighbors offer this gift to help ease your pain.
7. Many a time I have wished for riches; many a time my wishes were granted.
8. The endangered rivers included the Klamath River, Oregon; the Salmon River, Idaho; the Eel River, Northern California; and the Colorado River, Southern California.
9. Someone's in the kitchen with Dinah; someone's in the kitchen I know.
10. Cake is a wonderful dessert; especially, chocolate cake.

Colons

Page 40
Exercise A.
1. My favorite sports are baseball, volleyball, and soccer. **(no colon)**
2. The following are foods I like: hot dogs, chili beans, and cottage cheese.
3. The history lesson was about Columbus, settling of the Americas, and the displacement of Indians. **(no colon)**
4. We studied the following: Columbus, the settling of the Americas, and the displacement of Indians.
5. Here are the chapters we need to study: I, IV, and V.
6. It is said: A bird in the hand is worth two in the bush.
7. Above the counter loomed the sign: No shoes, no shirt, no service.

Exercise B.
1. 7:30 a.m.
2. 5:17
3. 11:47:05
4. 2:4 (flour to water)
5. I:3:23-30

Exercise C.
1. I'd say "yes" to almost any food right now; especially, hamburgers.
2. If you pass this test, you'll be a high ranker: someone who'll be hired very soon.
3. This program is dedicated to children's entertainment: face painting, juggling, and mime, to name a few.
4. We're interested in organizations involved in physical fitness activities; i.e., health clubs, sports, gymnastics.
5. The Old Country Inn's opening-day ceremony offers the following specials: two nights with room-service breakfast, $40.00; free dessert with dinner, first night; and all-you-can-eat buffet, second night.

Hyphens

Page 44
Exercise A.
1. three-year term
2. a term of three years
3. a comment off the record
4. an off-the-record comment
5. quiet-spoken person
6. a person who speaks quietly
7. a hero who is known well
8. a well-known hero
9. an accident-prone person
10. a person who is accident prone
11. sister-in-law
12. top coat
13. automobile
14. a write-in candidate
15. an ex-mayor
16. a 7-to-6 vote
17. one-half cup
18. biology
19. a run-on sentence
20. a poverty-stricken people
21. 40-hour week
22. 5-string banjo
23. U-boat
24. up-to-date license
25. in the wind
26. pre-Civil War
27. allied
28. all-inclusive
29. a hill-less landscape
30. the right time of the day
31. midship
32. exculpate
33. two-story house
34. un-Canadian
35. three-eighths
36. freight train
37. thirty-odd years old
38. halfback
39. half-baked idea
40. an A-frame house

Page 45
Exercise B.
1. a-lone   Guideline #3
2. shor-ten   Guideline #1
3. six-ty   Guideline #4
4. Shake-spearen   Guideline #5
5. o-boe   Guideline #3

Exercise C.
1. I'll re-cover the chair when I recover from the flu.
2. The baby was ill clothed for such cold weather.
3. Why would such a respected committee write such an off-the-wall report?
4. The graduates were 21-23 years old.
5. Stay tuned for up-to-the minute news.
6. The mill is hiring part-time employees.
7. Alicia and Elena are co-owners of the business.

8. How often have your parents had a heart-to-heart talk with you?
9. I received seventy-five cents in change.
10. Please change this ten-dollar bill into ten dollar bills.
11. Ex-presidents are quickly forgotten.
12. It is a well-known fact that two-thirds of the money was lost.
13. Is a self-made person self-confident?
14. Please re-address this envelope.
15. His happiness was short lived, because what he thought was a well-implemented plan was really an ill-conceived one.
16. My favorite program was pre-empted by a fast-breaking news event.
17. In our class eight-, nine-, and ten-year old gymnasts are grouped together.
18. Is it time for your mid-afternoon nap?
19. He turned down a $50,000-a-year salary.
20. We rented a 16-foot sailboat for a 3-week cruise.
21. The L-shaped living room is two-thirds the size of our family room.
22. Our son-in-law owns 10-15 different cars.
23. You can have a two-, three-, or four-year lease.
24. The drop-off slot is next to the self-closing door.
25. Who is the prime minister-elect?

Parentheses

Page 47
Exercise A.
1. I nearly called my accountants (Carter and Carter).
2. Complete this form (the one marked 1040A), and return it to this office.
3. Our committee has several objectives: (a) increase revenues, (b) increase membership, and (c) provide community service.
4. Please find an enclosed check for ten dollars ($10).
5. His call was prompt (within five minutes).
6. Parentheses are used to enclose (1) certain words, (2) certain phrases, and (3) numbers and letters.
7. In 1993, the Oregon Trail was marked with a sesquicentennial (150th) celebration.
8. He called last week (was it Friday?), but I was not here.

9. We can see a great change by comparing our income before 1980 (first chart) with our income after 1980 (second chart).
10. (Punctuate a separate sentence.) She did not try to answer. (She could not.)

Dashes

Page 50
Exercise A.
1. Tomorrow night I appear for the first time before a Boston audience—4000 critics.
   —Letter to Pamela Clemens Moffit
2. Put all your eggs in the one basket and—WATCH THAT BASKET.
   —*Pudd'nhead Wilson*
3. Each person is born to one possession which out values all his others—his last breath.
   —*Pudd'nhead Wilson*
4. Biographies are but the clothes and buttons of the man—the biography of the man himself cannot be written.
   —Autobiography
5. Adam was but human—this explains it all. He did not want the apple for the apple's sake, he wanted it only because it was forbidden.
   —*Pudd'nhead Wilson*
6. I do not want Michael Angelo—for break fast—for luncheon—for dinner—for tea—for supper—or between meals.
   —*Innocents Abroad*

Exercise B.
1. Yesterday, December 7, 1941–a day which will live in infamy–the United States of America was suddenly and deliberately attacked....
   —Franklin D. Roosevelt, Message to Congress
2. There is only one success–to be able to spend your life in your own way.
   —Christopher Morley, *Where the Blue Begins*
3. I don't think necessity is the mother of invention–invention, in my opinion, arises directly from idleness, possibly also from laziness.
   —Agatha Christie, *An Autobiography*

Page 51
Exercise C.

1. Public officials should act responsibly–not like bumbling fools.
2. Your clothes should be washed–the laundromat is open until midnight–and ironed.
3. "Funny thing—" he said, never completing his thought.
4. Tall timber, lush undergrowth, and abundant water–these things impress a first-time visitor to western Oregon.
5. After years of training, she achieved her goal–the chief executive officer of a large corporation.
6. I suppose you agree KOAP–AM–FM is an excellent public radio station.
7. Calculus, differential equations, statistics–my hardest courses are all math.
8. "Watch—watch out! The ladder is fall–!"
9. I will never–never, I say never–return to such an unfriendly business.
10. She was playing–I remember it well–with a friend in the rain.

Mid-Review Test, No.2

Page 52
Exercise A.

January 15, 1992

Jack Jones, Jr.
1122 Miramar Dr., #2
Santa Clara, Calif.

Dear Jack,

I'm planning a going-away party Sept. 17 for Ms. Stevens, who is joining the Peace Corps. Please let me know if you can attend, and I'll make preparations. By the way, could you lend me your copy of *American History Illustrated*, Vol. 27, Number 6? There's an article on Julia Ward Howe, the author of the "Battle Hymn of the Republic," that I'd like to read.

Thanks,

Jean

Exercise B.

1. Governor Johnson, a Democrat and family practitioner, supports the bill that bans smoking in a variety of locations—from video arcades to airport waiting rooms.

   or Governor Johnson (**a Democrat and family practitioner**). . .

2. The Military Park Hotel—see the before-and-after photos in your program—in Newark, New Jersey, was demolished by an implosion.

Exercise C.

This year's fundraiser to raise money to fight **multiple sclerosis** will be held at **M**ount (or **Mt.**) **H**ood **M**eadows. There will be volunteers at the site accepting **applications** for coaches for the Manitoba **Q**uad **A** baseball team.

Brackets

Page 54
Exercise A.

1. He said, "Boots and Max [both Manx cats] were found in our neighbor's back-yard."
2. He says Boots and Max (both Manx cats) were found in our neighbor's backyard.
3. My brother (the youngest of six children) is responsible for all morning chores.
4. The article told about life in "Phenix, Arizona [*sic*]" and "Memphis, Tenesee [*sic*]."
5. The sheriff (Gorge Diaz) has been elected to office seven times.
6. "The sheriff [Gorge Diaz] has been elected to office seven times."
7. "Ask what *you* can do for your country." [Emphasis added]
8. "In that year [1922], we had lived in Ontario and New York," his diary recorded.
9. "I will disperse a check for seven hundred dollars [$700] as quickly as possible."
10. "The act was a feet [*sic*] of dexterity and skill," the reviewer wrote.

Ellipses

Page 56
Exercise A.

"Four score and seven years ago our fathers brought forth on this continent a new nation, conceived in liberty and dedicated to the proposition that all men are created equal.

"Now we are engaged in a great civil war. . . . We are met on a great battlefield of that war. We have come to dedicate . . . that field as a final resting place for those who here gave their lives. . . . It is altogether fitting and proper that we should do this.

"But, in a larger sense, we cannot dedicate . . . this ground. The brave men, living and dead, who struggled here, have consecrated it far above our poor power to add or detract. The world . . . can never forget what they did here. It is for us the living, rather, to be dedicated here to the unfinished work which they who fought here have thus far so nobly advanced.

"It is rather for us to . . . resolve that these dead shall not have died in vain; that this nation, under God, shall have a new birth of freedom, and that government of the people, by the people, for the people, shall not perish from the earth."

Final Assessment Test

Pages 58 and 59
Exercise A.
1. message
2. *réponde s'il vous plait*
3. rest in peace
4. before Christ
5. Boulevard
6. April
7. annual percentage rate
8. medical doctor
9. Mobile Army Surgical Hospital
10. report

Exercise B.
1. "She'll Be Comin' 'Round the Mountain," is a song about a train.
2. When I start to argue, my father always says: "No if's, and's, or but's about it,"
3. "It's just your opinion, isn't it?" Emily queried.
4. Don't eat Dad's donut!
5. The brothers did each other's chores.

Exercise C.
1. Kids will be entertained this Sunday during the 8th Annual Asian Celebration being held at the Lane County Fairgrounds. The official opening will begin with a colorful Chinese lion. Japanese drumming by the Eugene City Taiko—a local troupe—will follow.

2. In an extraordinary collaboration by Detroit's automakers, General Motors, Ford, and Chrysler are discussing building jointly an electric car; therefore, meeting the requirements of the clean-ir law first enacted in California.

3. Dear Mr. Johnson:
    I'll be your "Big Brother" at Mt. Loyola College, which you plan to attend in the fall. The following items may be useful: a tape recorder, a lap-top computer, and a printer. Please be at Allen Hall at 9:30 a.m. sharp. The lecture will center around an article in *Global Science Magazine* (a.k.a., *GSM*), vol. 253(1):45-52, 1989. The title is "The Manatee: Its Habitat and Habits." Remember: promptness is not only important to the lecturer; it is also important to you.
    Sincerely, John Tubbs

4. The weather service office in New York City put the storm's size in perspective. By the time snow was expected to start in the city (around dawn Saturday), the center of the storm would still be over western Ontario —some 700 miles away.

Exercise D.
1. **Twelve** people purchased tickets to the lecture entitled "Travels Through Europe."
2. I have better-than-average grades this semester.
3. He is a member of the United Auto Workers (UAW).
4. Elena, my younger daughter, enters school next year.
5. These party favors—they cost less than a dollar—are available at the card shop.

STRAIGHT FORWARD ENGLISH SERIES

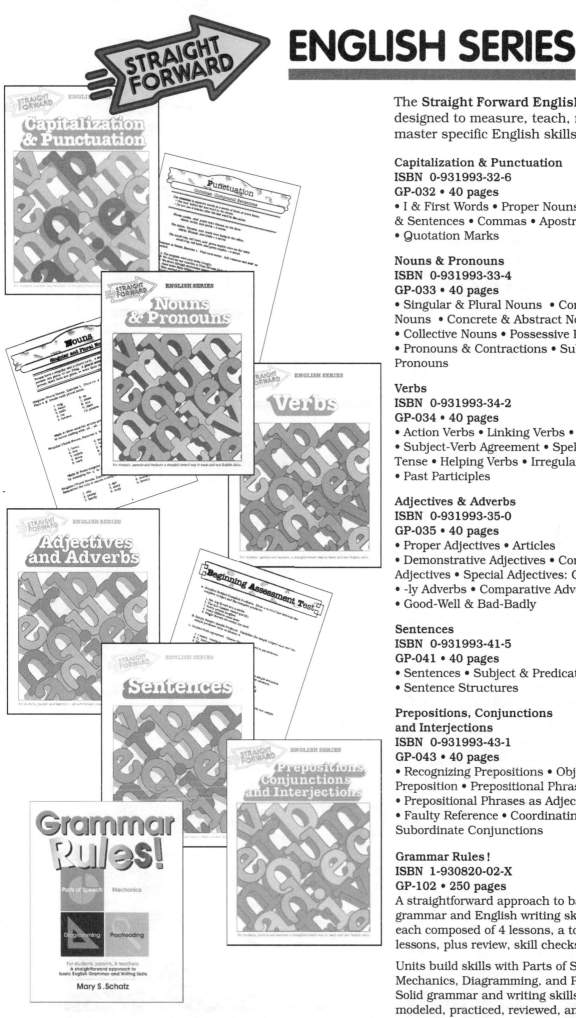

The **Straight Forward English Series** is designed to measure, teach, review, and master specific English skills.

Capitalization & Punctuation
ISBN 0-931993-32-6
GP-032 • 40 pages
• I & First Words • Proper Nouns • Ending Marks & Sentences • Commas • Apostrophes
• Quotation Marks

Nouns & Pronouns
ISBN 0-931993-33-4
GP-033 • 40 pages
• Singular & Plural Nouns • Common & Proper Nouns • Concrete & Abstract Nouns
• Collective Nouns • Possessive Pronouns
• Pronouns & Contractions • Subject & Objective Pronouns

Verbs
ISBN 0-931993-34-2
GP-034 • 40 pages
• Action Verbs • Linking Verbs • Verb Tense
• Subject-Verb Agreement • Spelling Rules for Tense • Helping Verbs • Irregular Verbs
• Past Participles

Adjectives & Adverbs
ISBN 0-931993-35-0
GP-035 • 40 pages
• Proper Adjectives • Articles
• Demonstrative Adjectives • Comparative Adjectives • Special Adjectives: Good & Bad
• -ly Adverbs • Comparative Adverbs
• Good-Well & Bad-Badly

Sentences
ISBN 0-931993-41-5
GP-041 • 40 pages
• Sentences • Subject & Predicate
• Sentence Structures

Prepositions, Conjunctions and Interjections
ISBN 0-931993-43-1
GP-043 • 40 pages
• Recognizing Prepositions • Object of the Preposition • Prepositional Phrases
• Prepositional Phrases as Adjectives & Adverbs
• Faulty Reference • Coordinating, Correlative & Subordinate Conjunctions

Grammar Rules!
ISBN 1-930820-02-X
GP-102 • 250 pages
A straightforward approach to basic English grammar and English writing skills. Forty units each composed of 4 lessons, a total of 160 lessons, plus review, skill checks, and answers.

Units build skills with Parts of Speech, Mechanics, Diagramming, and Proofreading. Solid grammar and writing skills are explained, modeled, practiced, reviewed, and tested.

The **Large Editions** of the **Advanced Straight Forward English Series** are for higher level English skills.

Clauses & Phrases
ISBN 0-931993-55-5
GP-055 • 80 pages
• Adverb, Adjective & Noun Clauses • Gerund, Participial & Infinitive Verbals • Gerund, Participial, Infinitive, Prepositional & Appositive Phrases

Mechanics
ISBN 0-931993-56-3
GP-056 • 80 pages
• Abbreviations • Apostrophes • Capitalization
• Italics • Quotation Marks • Numbers
• Commas • Semicolons • Colons • Hyphens
• Parentheses • Dashes • Brackets • Ellipses
• Slashes

Grammar & Diagramming Sentences
ISBN 0-931993-75-X
GP-075 • 110 pages
• The Basics • Diagramming Rules & Patterns
• Nouns & Pronouns • Verbs • Modifiers
• Prepositions, Conjunctions, and Special Items
• Clauses & Compound-Complex Sentences

Troublesome Grammar
ISBN 0-931993-19-9
GP-019 • 120 pages
• Agreement • Regular & Irregular Verbs
• Modifiers • Prepositions & Case
• Posssessives & Contractions • Plurals
• Active & Passive Voice • Comparative Forms
• Word Usage • and more.

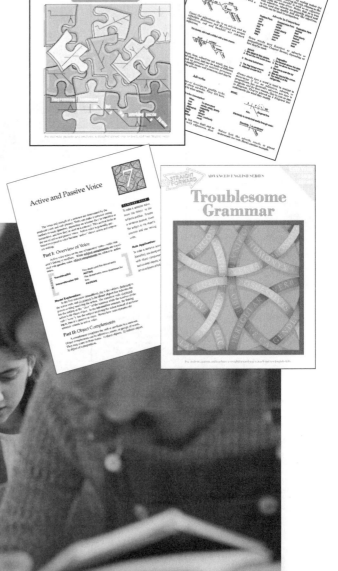